The London Coffee Guide.

2015

D1335232

Edited by
Jeffrey Young
and Guy Simpson

Author: Allegra Strategies
Photography: Kate Beard, Maximilian Gower,
Joan Torrelles and Warattaya S. Bullôt
Design: John Osborne
Website: Tim Spring
Publisher: Allegra Publications Ltd

Allegra
PUBLICATIONS

Visit our website:
www.londoncoffeeguide.com

🐦 **@ldncoffeeguide**

All information was accurate at time of going to press.

Published by *Allegra* PUBLICATIONS Ltd © 2015

Walkden House, 10 Melton Street, London, NW1 2EB

Foreword

by **Laura Harper-Hinton**, Co-Owner Caravan Restaurants, Caravan Coffee Roasters

Our first restaurant and coffee roasting business celebrated its fifth birthday last month. Five wonderful, 'hardyard' years in the London coffee and dining scene. These moments always give you an opportunity to look back and remember, not so fondly, the two-year agonising search for a site as an unproven concept. And, after finally finding that site, we can still recall the favour begging, brick lugging and penny pinching to get our Exmouth Market venue open. It made me think, with an eye to the future, about the business of specialty coffee in the UK.

Having worked growing up in some of New Zealand's pioneering roasteries of the eighties, it is amazing to reflect on how far London and the UK has come in a very short space of time. London is now one of the most innovative, evolving and quality-driven specialty coffee markets in the world, something I never would have thought possible fourteen years ago when I first arrived here.

What then does this mean for the business of specialty coffee in the UK? Consumers increasingly want a coffee experience that is defined by the integrity and quality of the product, but also attention to detail, beautiful design and a unique experience. As our business now reaches out to a wider audience than ever before, the challenge is to stay true to our core values and not steer into the realms of the ordinary which we set ourselves apart from in the first place.

With more and more coffee shops, all-day restaurants and coffee roasteries opening in London all the time, there is now an imperative for all of us in this industry to support each other in the name of the greater cause – specialty coffee. Come join us, there is a lot more work to be done.

Contents

Introduction

Welcome to The London Coffee Guide 2015 – the definitive guide to London's independent coffee venues.

The Guide was born out of a desire to find the best and most interesting places to go for coffee in London. Following a boom in new openings since the first edition of the Guide in 2011, London is now home to a thriving, world-class independent coffee scene. The 2015 edition profiles 185 venues, an increase on the 150 featured last year, reflecting this exciting growth.

This book aims to assist and inform people who are keen to explore this vibrant city in a quest for fantastic coffee venues. We all visit cafés for different reasons: for many, coffee itself is the main attraction, for some, it's the buzz of visiting a unique coffee shop. Others go for the opportunity to relax, socialise or conduct business. Whatever your motivation, our objective is to encourage you to try something different and discover places you otherwise might never have known.

In this edition we have expanded the Coffee Knowledge chapter with two additional articles on the subjects of espresso, and the importance of coffee education. We would like to thank all the industry experts for contributing their knowledge to help readers learn more about and experiment with the coffee they love.

Allegra is an established leader in consumer and business intelligence for the coffee industry in the UK and Europe. We have drawn on this research as well as experts in the field to compile this edition. We hope you enjoy it.

About the Guide

Ratings

Every venue featured in The London Coffee Guide 2015 has been visited and rated by our expert team. The ratings fall into two distinct categories: Coffee Rating and Overall Rating on a score of 1-5, with 5 being the highest possible score. Customer feedback received via The London Coffee Guide website and app also informs the venue shortlist and the final scores.

Coffee Rating

The Coffee Rating is about much more than just taste in the cup. An excellent coffee experience depends on a host of factors including: barista skills, coffee supplier, equipment, consistency, working processes and coffee presentation. The venue's coffee philosophy and commitment to excellence are also taken into consideration.

Overall Rating

In combination with the Coffee Rating, the Overall Rating reflects the total coffee shop experience for the customer. Factors taken into account include: service, café ambience, venue scale and impact, design and food quality. Feedback from the industry is also taken into consideration.

The Guide includes coffee carts and kiosks, as well as coffee shops. It was not considered fair to compare these venues with permanent cafés, so these venues have not been rated. The best carts, stalls and kiosks are grouped together in a separate chapter.

Key to symbols

Roaster

Alternative brew methods available

Coffee beans sold on site

Gluten-free products available

Venue has a loyalty card

Soya milk available

Toilets

Parent & baby friendly

Disabled access

Wifi available

Licensed

Coffee courses available

Outdoor seating

Brunch available at weekends

Venues marked as are new to this edition of the Guide.

A Brief History of London Coffee Shops

THE EARLY YEARS

800 AD The coffee plant (Coffea) attracts human interest and consumption as early as 800 AD in the Kaffe region of Ethiopia. According to legend, it was an Ethiopian goat herder named Kaldi who first discovered how animated his herd of goats became after chewing on the red berries.

MID 17TH CENTURY

Travellers to Middle Eastern areas such as the Ottoman Empire bring coffee to Europe and Britain.

1650 The first English coffee house is established in Oxford by a Jewish gentleman named Jacob at the Angel in the parish of St Peter.

Coffee houses become meeting places for political and literary debates between artists, intellectuals, merchants and bankers. Such venues are known as Penny Universities, in reference to the one penny entrance fee. They are closely associated with reading and provide pamphlets and newspapers, as well as copious amounts of coffee.

1652 London's first coffee house is established by Pasqua Rosée in St Michael's Alley, Cornhill, London EC3.

1668 Edward Lloyd's Coffee House in Lombard Street becomes a key meeting place for ship owners and marine insurance brokers. Situated on the site occupied by Lloyds bank today, this coffee house likely contributed to London becoming a global hub for insurance and financial services.

1674 The Women's Petition Against Coffee is set up in London in response to men spending less time at home due to the "excessive use of the drying and enfeebling liquor".

1675 There are now more than 3,000 coffee houses across England. King Charles II attempts to outlaw coffee houses as hotbeds of revolution, but following large public protests, his proclamation is revoked after 11 days.

1680 Jonathan's Coffee House is established by Jonathan Miles in Change Alley. It is a place where stockbrokers frequently meet and eventually becomes today's London Stock Exchange.

1706 Thomas Twining opens the first known tea room in London, which can still be found at 216 Strand.

18TH CENTURY

Coffee houses gradually decline in popularity and become more elite establishments, when they start charging more than one penny for entrance. Travelling taverns replace coffee houses as popular social spaces. Coffee also becomes a less important commodity as the East India Company and British trade in general focuses more on tea imports from India.

LAST CENTURY

1894 Lyons opens a chain of tea rooms followed by Lyons Corner Houses in London's West End in 1906.

1923 The Kenya Coffee Company Limited (Kenco) is established and soon begins selling coffee on Vere Street, Mayfair.

1950s Italian-run espresso houses featuring Formica-topped tables are a popular feature of this era, particularly in London's Soho.

1952 Moka Bar opens on Frith Street and is London's first espresso bar.

1971 Starbucks opens its first store at Pike Place Market in Seattle, USA.

First Costa Coffee shop opened by brothers Sergio and Bruno Costa at 9 Newport Street, London.

1978 An early pioneer of artisanal coffee, Monmouth Coffee Company opens in Monmouth Street, Covent Garden.

1986 Pret A Manger is established by college friends Julian Metcalf and Sinclair Beecham.

1992 Fairtrade Foundation is established in London by the Catholic Overseas Development Agency, Christian Aid, Oxfam, Traidcraft, the World Development Movement, and the National Federation of Women's Institutes.

1995 Whitbread Group acquires Costa Coffee with 41 stores and a roastery in Lambeth.

1997 Nescafé opens first Café Nescafé trial stores in London and UK, but closes all outlets several years later.

Gerry Ford acquires five Caffè Nero stores and begins building a chain, which grows to become the third-largest coffee shop brand in the UK.

1998 Starbucks launches in the UK, acquiring 65 Seattle Coffee Company stores for an estimated £52 million.

1999 Allegra Strategies releases the groundbreaking Project Café Report, which predicts a significant boom in coffee shops.

LAST DECADE

2000 Internet cafés grow in popularity during the dotcom era.

Marks & Spencer launches Café Revive concept.

2001 The caffè latte is added to the Consumer Price Index (CPI), the basket of goods the government uses to measure products purchased by a typical British household.

2005 Flat White coffee shop opens in Berwick Street, Soho, setting the stage for further Antipodean influences on coffee in the UK.

2006 The number of branded chain coffee shop outlets exceeds 1,000 in London alone.

2007 James Hoffmann is crowned World Barista Champion and founds Square Mile Coffee Roasters.

2008 The first-ever European Coffee Symposium is held at London's Park Lane Hotel.

2009 A host of new artisanal "third wave" coffee shops open in London.

The UK's Gwilym Davies is crowned World Barista Champion.

2010 Costa, Starbucks and several other mainstream coffee chains launch their versions of the flat white.

The World Barista Championships are held in London at Caffè Culture.

The first edition of The London Coffee Guide is published.

2011 Growth of artisanal coffee shops and micro coffee roasteries in London continues to accelerate with the arrival of Workshop (formerly St. Ali), and Prufrock Coffee.

First-ever London Coffee Festival held at the Old Truman Brewery on Brick Lane.

2012 Roastery/cafés increase in popularity with the opening of Caravan King's Cross, Ozone and TAP Wardour Street.

London Coffee Festival hosts UK Barista Championship finals.

Harris + Hoole opens first London store.

2013 Bulldog Edition opens at Ace Hotel London, in collaboration with Square Mile Coffee Roasters.

2014 The London Coffee Festival is attended by over 22,000 visitors.

Growth of speciality mini-chains, with leading independents such as Grind & Co and Workshop Coffee Co. opening multiple new sites.

Maxwell Colonna-Dashwood wins the UK Barista Championship for the second time.

West End

London's West End is synonymous with the city's legendary theatre and music scene, as well as its restaurants, shopping and nightlife. Business people and actors rub shoulders with tourists and urbanites, and the area's café culture is just as diverse.

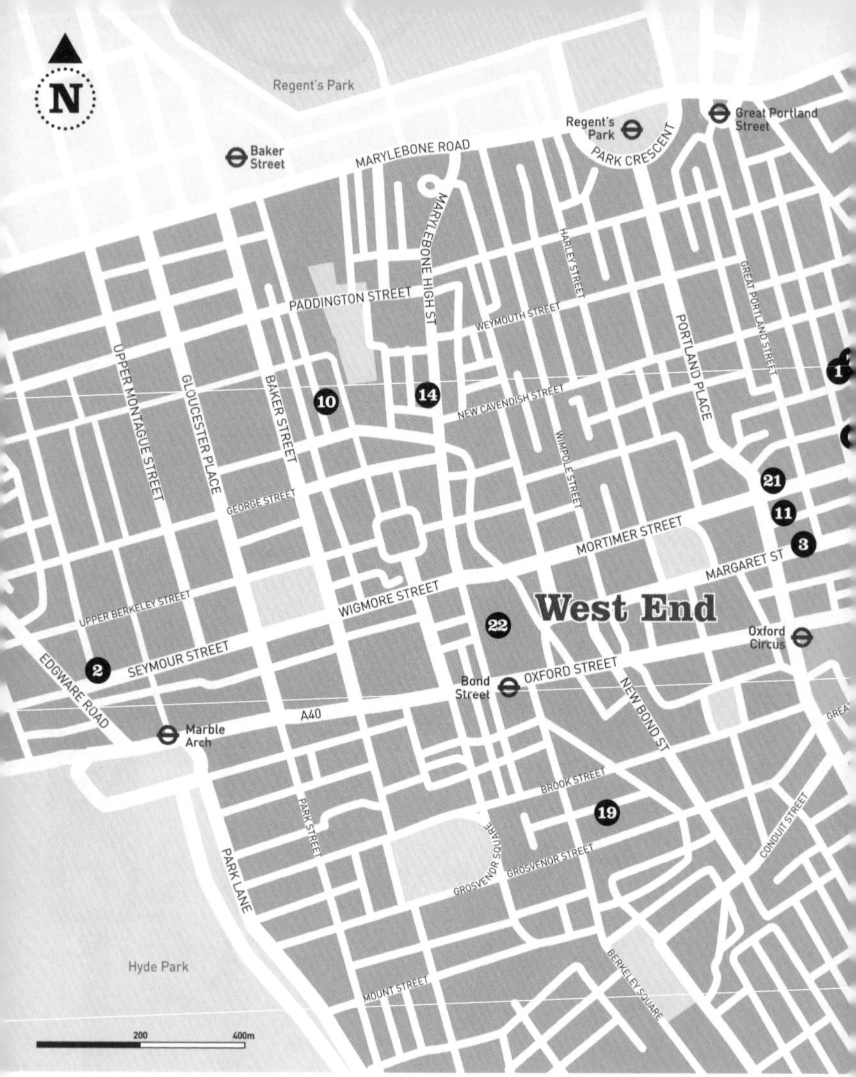

N
Regent's Park
Baker Street
MARYLEBONE ROAD
Regent's Park
PARK CRESCENT
Great Portland Street
MARYLEBONE HIGH ST
HARLEY STREET
GREAT PORTLAND STREET
PADDINGTON STREET
WEYMOUTH STREET
PORTLAND PLACE
UPPER MONTAGUE STREET
GLOUCESTER PLACE
BAKER STREET
NEW CAVENDISH STREET
WIMPOLE STREET
GEORGE STREET
MORTIMER STREET
MARGARET ST
WIGMORE STREET
UPPER BERKELEY STREET
West End
Oxford Circus
SEYMOUR STREET
EDGWARE ROAD
Bond Street
OXFORD STREET
NEW BOND ST
A40
Marble Arch
BROOK STREET
PARK STREET
PARK LANE
GROSVENOR SQUARE
GROSVENOR STREET
CONDUIT STREET
Hyde Park
BERKELEY SQUARE
MOUNT STREET
200
400m
1
2
3
10
11
14
19
21
22

COFFEE VENUES KEY

West End

1 The Attendant p4
2 The Borough Barista p4
3 Curators Coffee Gallery p5 * ◊
4 Department of Coffee and Social Affairs (Covent Garden) p6 *
5 Fernandez & Wells (Somerset House) p6
6 Kaffeine p7 ◊
7 Kin Cafe p8 *
8 Lantana (Fitzrovia) p9
9 Monmouth Coffee Company (Covent Garden) p10
10 Monocle Café p11
11 Mother's Milk p12 *
12 New Row Coffee p13
13 Notes (Trafalgar Square) p13 ◊
14 The Providores and Tapa Room p14
15 Sharps Coffee Bar p14 ◊
16 Store Street Espresso p15 ◊
17 TAP Coffee (Rathbone Place) p16
18 TAP Coffee (Tottenham Court Road) p17
19 Taylor St Baristas (Mayfair) p18
20 Timberyard (Seven Dials) p19
21 Workshop Coffee Co. (Fitzrovia) p20 * ◊
22 Workshop Coffee Co. (Marylebone) p21

* NEW
◊ TOP 30

The Attendant

27a Foley Street, W1W 6DY

The Attendant is a coffee bar sited in a former Victorian public lavatory. This astonishing conversion has artfully preserved several original features. Suffice to say that the cups and saucers are not the only porcelain the visitor will encounter. Caravan coffee is accompanied by a mouth-watering array of New York deli style sandwiches, which can be ordered through the toilet attendant's old window. Don't be shy to spend a penny or two at one of London's most original coffee venues.

+44(0)20 7637 3794
www.the-attendant.com
⊖ Goodge Street / Oxford Circus

MON–FRI. 8:00am - 6:00pm
SAT. 9:00am - 6:00pm
SUN. 10:00am - 5:00pm

First opened 2013
Roaster Caravan
Machine La Marzocco GB/5, 2 groups
Grinder Mazzer Robur E

Espresso £2.20
Cappuccino £2.80
Latte £2.80
Flat white £2.80

MAP REF. **1**

COFFEE 4.50 / 5 — **OVERALL** 4.25 / 5

The Borough Barista

60 Seymour Street, W1H 7JN

Borough Barista provides an artisanal alternative to the high street chains that predominate in West London. This venue provides a calm oasis of blonde wood and friendly service just around the corner from Marble Arch. The large downstairs seating area provides ample space for a business meeting, or to spread out with the Saturday papers. The chocolaty 'St James' espresso blend is custom roasted for Borough Barista, and enjoyed in crisp surroundings by a smart Mayfair crowd.

+44(0)20 7563 7222
www.theboroughbarista.com
⊖ Marble Arch

MON–SAT. 8:00am - 5:30pm
SUN. Closed

First opened 2011
Roaster Union Hand-Roasted custom blend
Machine La Marzocco Linea, 2 groups
Grinder Mazzer Super Jolly, Eureka

Espresso £1.80 / £2.00
Cappuccino £2.60 / £3.00
Latte £2.60 / £3.00
Flat white £2.60 / £3.00

MAP REF. **2**

COFFEE 4.00 / 5 — **OVERALL** 4.25 / 5

Curators Coffee Gallery

51 Margaret Street, W1W 8SG

The interior of this Fitzrovia venue dares to deviate from the bare brick and distressed furnishings seen in so many London independents. There is dark wood, a pristine white bar and kettles made from blazing copper. Spectacular signature drinks such as iced Cascara make neat additions to an already appealing coffee selection. The Curators Coffee Gallery, as the name suggests, is a place to settle in and escape with coffee and art. Whether it's artistry in the cup, on the walls, or indeed on the cup itself, this is a unique coffee shop with a vitality which goes way beyond just the coffee.

+44(0)20 7580 2547
www.curatorscoffee.com
⊖ Oxford Circus

Sister locations Curators Coffee Studio

MON–FRI. 7:30am – 6:30pm
SAT–SUN. 9:00am – 6:00pm

First opened 2014
Roaster Nude Espresso and guests
Machine La Marzocco Strada EP, 3 groups
Grinder Mahlkönig K 30 x2, Mahlkönig EK 43

Espresso £2.20
Cappuccino £2.80
Latte £2.80
Flat white £2.80

MAP REF. **3**

5

Department of Coffee and Social Affairs

Covent Garden 19 Slingsby Place, St. Martins Courtyard, WC2E 9AB

The polished design of Department of Coffee and Social Affairs' newest store befits its fashionable Covent Garden location. The café's elegant red awning shades an al fresco seating area with prime views over the elegant shops of St. Martin's Courtyard. The coffee here is similarly refined, with two single origin coffees for espresso-based drinks and two roasts for filter. A scrumptious array of neatly presented sandwiches lead the lunch menu, the perfect start to a hard-earned afternoon hitting the boutiques.

www.departmentofcoffee.com
⊖ Leicester Square / Covent Garden

Sister locations Leather Lane / Chancery Lane / Carnaby Street / Piccadilly / Norton Folgate

MON–FRI. 8:00am - 7:00pm
SAT. 9:30am - 7:00pm
SUN. 11:00am - 7:00pm

First opened 2015
Roaster Department of Coffee and Social Affairs
Machine La Marzocco Linea PB, 3 groups
Grinder Mazzer Robur E, Mazzer Super Jolly, Mahlkönig Tanzania

Espresso £2.40
Cappuccino £2.90
Latte £2.90
Flat white £2.70   **MAP REF.** ❹

COFFEE 4.50 / 5		OVERALL 4.50 / 5	

Fernandez & Wells Somerset House

Somerset House, Strand, WC2R 1LA

This prestigious venue occupies three rooms in one of London's most beautiful buildings. Customers are treated to the very best of everything: Sicilian panettone, Amalfi lemons, the finest meats, cheeses and European wines... the list goes on. At the beating heart of the operation is a Synesso Cyncra, handled by a skilled team of baristas who also prepare delicate single estate filter coffees. This is more than a café - it is a fine food and coffee emporium.

+44(0)20 7420 9408
www.fernandezandwells.com
⊖ Temple

Sister locations Beak Street / Denmark Street / Lexington Street / South Kensington / Duke Street

MON–FRI. 8:00am - 10:00pm
SAT. 10:00am - 10:00pm
SUN. 10:00am - 8:00pm

First opened 2011
Roaster Has Bean bespoke blend
Machine Synesso Cyncra, 3 groups
Grinder Mazzer Robur E x2, Mahlkönig Tanzania

Espresso £2.40
Cappuccino £2.80
Latte £2.80
Flat white £2.80

MAP REF. ❺

COFFEE 4.25 / 5		OVERALL 4.50 / 5	

Kaffeine

66 Great Titchfield Street, W1W 7QJ

Since opening in 2009, Kaffeine has established itself as one of London's pre-eminent coffee venues. Australian Owner Peter Dore-Smith sets the bar high and his team strives to provide the best experience possible for all, from casual lunch customers to coffee experts. This café is distinguished by its impeccable attention to detail, from the stylish wooden interior to the food made fresh on site. Kaffeine has developed a loyal following and remains a source of inspiration for London's coffee community. A hotly anticipated sister store, sited on nearby Eastcastle Street, is due to open in spring 2015.

+44(0)20 7580 6755
www.kaffeine.co.uk
⊖ Oxford Circus

Sister locations Kaffeine (Eastcastle Street)

MON-FRI. 7:30am – 6:00pm
SAT. 8:30am – 6:00pm
SUN. 9:00am – 5:00pm

First opened 2009
Roaster Square Mile Coffee Roasters
Machine Synesso Cyncra, 3 groups
Grinder Mazzer Robur E, Anfim

Espresso £2.00 / £2.50
Cappuccino £2.90
Latte £2.90
Flat white £2.80

MAP REF. 6

Kin Cafe

22 Foley Street, W1W 6DT

Everything from the food to the furniture furthers Kin's mission to source in an ethical and socially responsible way. Their sourdough bread, for example, is baked by Better Health Bakery, an East London social enterprise employing adults recovering from mental illness. Kin's soothing interior of clean lines and muted tones falls somewhere between a Scandinavian kitchen and Japanese tea room. It's an environment to calm the soul, providing a serene backdrop to the sumptuous menu of superfood salads, quiche, cakes and baked goodies.

+44(0)20 7998 4720
www.kincafe.co.uk
Goodge Street / Oxford Circus

MON-FRI. 8:00am - 6:00pm
SAT. 10:00am - 4:00pm
SUN. Closed

First opened 2014
Roaster Notes Roastery and guests
Machine La Marzocco Linea, 2 groups
Grinder Anfim, Mahlkönig EK 43

Espresso £2.20
Cappuccino £2.60 / £2.90
Latte £2.60 / £2.90
Flat white £2.60

MAP REF. **7**

COFFEE 4.25 / 5
OVERALL 4.25 / 5

Lantana Fitzrovia

13 Charlotte Place, W1T 1SN

Stylish and understated Fitzrovia favourite Lantana has gone from strength to strength since opening in 2008. This café and eatery is always abuzz with chatter and filled with loyal patrons, particularly during the weekend when its legendary brunch menu has customers queuing out the door. The coffee here is of a consistently high quality, both on the main premises and at the second shopfront next door that caters just for takeaway traffic.

+44(0)20 7637 3347
www.lantanacafe.co.uk
⊖ Goodge Street / Tottenham Court Road

Sister locations Shoreditch / Camden

MON. 8:00am - 6:00pm
TUE-FRI. 8:00am - 9:30pm
SAT-SUN. 9:00am - 5:00pm

First opened 2008
Roaster Alchemy bespoke blend
Machine La Marzocco Linea, 3 groups
Grinder Mazzer Robur E, Anfim

Espresso £2.00
Cappuccino £2.60
Latte £2.60
Flat white £2.60

MAP REF.

COFFEE 4.50 / 5	🫘🫘🫘🫘◗	OVERALL 4.50 / 5	★★★★⯪

Monmouth Coffee Company Covent Garden

27 Monmouth Street, WC2H 9EU

This is where the Monmouth phenomenon began, back in 1978. The original Monmouth roastery occupied this site until 2007 when it moved to Bermondsey. The interior here is simple, focusing attention on the coffee. Wooden booths encourage strangers to share conversation and trade ideas, continuing the grand tradition of the capital's first coffee houses. Monmouth Coffee is nothing short of a London institution, and more often than not, queues snake out of the door, but it's definitely worth the wait.

+44(0)20 7232 3010
www.monmouthcoffee.co.uk
⊖ Covent Garden

Sister locations Borough / Bermondsey

MON–SAT. 8:00am – 6:30pm
SUN. Closed

First opened 1978
Roaster Monmouth Coffee Company
Machine La Marzocco Linea, 3 groups
Grinder Mazzer Robur E

Espresso £1.50
Cappuccino £2.50
Latte £2.50
Flat white £2.50

MAP REF. **9**

COFFEE 4.50 / 5   OVERALL 4.50 / 5

Monocle Café

18 Chiltern Street, W1U 7QA

Monocle Café is an impeccably curated coffee shop belonging to Tyler Brûlé's global current affairs, business and lifestyle magazine. The café bears all the hallmarks of Monocle's slick aspirational brand and design-conscious outlook. Every item is meticulously sourced, from the midcentury-style furniture, right down to the teaspoons and barista aprons. A small kitchen downstairs serves up plates of elegant fare, but it's the Swedish cinnamon buns and Japanese cakes that really steal the show.

+44(0)20 7135 2040
cafe.monocle.com
⊖ Baker Street

MON–FRI. 7:00am – 7:00pm
SAT–SUN. 8:00am – 7:00pm

First opened 2013
Roaster Allpress Espresso
Machine La Marzocco Linea PB, 2 groups
Grinder Mazzer Robur, Mazzer Super Jolly

Espresso £2.50
Cappuccino £3.00
Latte £3.00
Flat white £3.00

MAP REF.

COFFEE 4.00 / 5 🫘🫘🫘🫘🫘

OVERALL 4.25 / 5 ★★★★⯪

Mother's Milk

12 Little Portland Street, W1W 8BJ

Don't go to Mother's Milk expecting a trendy, artfully distressed artisan espresso bar. What you will find, however, is exceptionally good espresso made by two witty baristas in a space barely larger than a minicab booth. It's likely you'll find customers staring in awe at the revered Victoria Arduino machine as it gives birth to their coffee, ushered into the world by the skilled hand of James Wise or Will Hilliard. This place engenders a childlike rediscovery of the warming joys a cup of coffee can bring, unhindered by all the accoutrements we've come to expect.

www.mothersmilkcoffee.com
Oxford Circus

MON-FRI. 7:30am - 4:00pm
SAT-SUN. Closed

First opened 2013
Roaster JB Kaffee
Machine Victoria Arduino Athena Leva, 2 groups
Grinder Anfim, Mahlkönig Guatemala

Espresso £3.00
Cappuccino £3.00
Latte £3.00
Flat white £3.00

MAP REF. **11**

COFFEE
4.50 / 5

OVERALL
4.00 / 5
★★★★☆

New Row Coffee

24 New Row, WC2N 4LA

This miniature coffee house is staffed by super friendly coffee obsessives who discuss latte art in their downtime and prepare the best flat white on a street crammed with other outlets. Daily filter options are available at the bar, along with an enticing lemon drizzle cake, gourmet cookies and a range of pastries and sandwiches. Fresh almond milk is prepared each day, and the pulp is used to make tasty almond biscuits.

+44(0)20 3583 6949
www.newrowcoffee.co.uk
⊖ Leicester Square / Charing Cross

Sister locations FreeState Coffee

MON–FRI. 7:30am – 7:00pm
SAT–SUN. 9:00am – 7:00pm

First opened 2011
Roaster Union Hand-Roasted and guests
Machine La Marzocco Linea, 3 groups
Grinder Mazzer Robur, Mazzer Super Jolly

Espresso £2.20
Cappuccino £2.60
Latte £2.60
Flat white £2.60

MAP REF. **12**

 **COFFEE** 4.25 / 5 **OVERALL** 4.00 / 5  ★ ★ ★ ★ ☆

Notes Trafalgar Square

TOP 30

31 St Martin's Lane, WC2N 4ER

Notes Trafalgar Square was the first venue opened by Brazilian coffee entrepreneur Fabio Ferreira. Occupying a stunning room with high ceilings, large mirrors and a refined yet welcoming atmosphere, this is a coffee house that looks to London's past for its decor but is distinctly forward-looking in its coffee philosophy. The progressive coffee menu is complemented by a range of fine foods. In the evening, the café transforms into a wine bar, and theatre-goers in the know drop by to sample the range of excellent wines, spirits, cheeses and charcuterie.

+44(0)20 7240 0424
www.notes-uk.co.uk
⊖ Charing Cross / Leicester Square

Sister locations Moorgate

MON–WED. 7:30am – 9:00pm
THU–FRI. 7:30am – 10:00pm
SAT. 9:00am – 10:00pm
SUN. 10:00am – 6:00pm

First opened 2010
Roaster Notes Roastery
Machine La Marzocco Strada, 3 groups
Grinder Mazzer Robur, Mahlkönig EK 43

Espresso £2.20 / £2.40
Cappuccino £2.80
Latte £2.80
Flat white £2.80

MAP REF. **13**

 **COFFEE** 4.75 / 5 **OVERALL** 4.50 / 5  ★ ★ ★ ★ ½

The Providores and Tapa Room

109 Marylebone High Street, W1U 4RX

Run by New Zealand chef Peter Gordon, The Providores and Tapa Room is a fusion restaurant, café and wine bar with a distinct South Pacific flavour. The ground floor Tapa room features a huge Rarotongan tapa cloth on one wall and heaves with people at breakfast, while the dining room upstairs caters for a more formal lunch and dinner crowd. Coffee is supplied by up-and-coming roastery Volcano Coffee Works, the perfect accompaniment to a delicious brunch at this popular venue.

+44(0)20 7935 6175
www.theprovidores.co.uk
⊖ Baker Street / Bond Street

Sister locations Kopapa

MON-FRI. 8:30am - 11:00pm
SAT. 9:00am - 11:00pm
SUN. 9:00am - 10:30pm

First opened 2001
Roaster Volcano Coffee Works
Machine La Marzocco GB/5, 2 groups
Grinder Mazzer Super Jolly

Espresso £2.00 / £2.40
Cappuccino £3.00
Latte £3.00
Flat white £3.00

MAP REF. **14**

COFFEE 4.00 / 5 **OVERALL** 4.25 / 5 ★★★★✩

Sharps Coffee Bar

TOP 30

9 Windmill Street, W1T 2JF

At Sharps, a barber shop and coffee bar complement one another without a whisker of encroachment. Sharps is one of the few coffee shops to offer coffee from celebrated Berlin roastery, The Barn, and also offers guest coffees on every last week of the month. The café feels very neatly pulled together as a whole; every detail from the trim tiling to clean-cut branding befits this dapper Fitzrovia location.

+44(0)20 7636 8688
www.sharpsbarbers.com
⊖ Goodge Street

MON-FRI. 8:00am - 6:00pm
SAT. 10:00am - 6:00pm
SUN. 12:00am - 6:00pm

First opened 2013
Roaster The Barn and guests
Machine Kees van der Westen Spirit, 3 groups
Grinder Mahlkönig K 30, Mahlkönig EK 43

Espresso £2.00
Cappuccino £2.40
Latte £2.60
Flat white £2.40

MAP REF. **15**

COFFEE 4.50 / 5 **OVERALL** 4.50 / 5 ★★★★✩

Store Street Espresso

40 Store Street, WC1E 7DB

West End

This exciting venue joined the burgeoning foodie scene on Store Street in 2010 and crowds of hungry students and creatives have been flocking here ever since for the great coffee and electric atmosphere. The café itself is stylish and light-filled, with an ambience that encourages customers to linger for leisure, study or work. A passionate team of baristas serve Square Mile coffee on a Synesso Hydra, and regularly offer guest coffees from up-and-coming roasters such as Leeds' North Star.

www.storestespresso.co.uk
⊖ Goodge Street

MON-FRI. 7:30am - 7:00pm
SAT. 9:00am - 6:00pm
SUN. 10:00am - 5:00pm

First opened 2010
Roaster Square Mile Coffee Roasters
Machine Synesso Hydra, 2 groups
Grinder Mazzer Robur E,
Nuova Simonelli Mythos

Espresso £2.00 / £2.20
Cappuccino £2.60
Latte £2.60
Flat white £2.60

MAP REF. **16**

COFFEE 4.50 / 5	OVERALL 4.50 / 5

TAP Coffee Rathbone Place

26 Rathbone Place, W1T 1JD

TAP Coffee was one of the first London coffee bars to break with convention and offer a selection of different espresso blends. The venue's design theme blends burnished wood and steel with attractive features such as a Belfast sink filled with chilled drinks, and the classic delivery bicycle parked at the door. The Rathbone Place store is a popular hangout for Fitzrovia admen, who mastermind advertising campaigns over perfectly-poured flat whites.

+44(0)20 7580 2163
www.tapcoffee.co.uk
⊖ Tottenham Court Road / Goodge Street

Sister locations Tottenham Court Road / Wardour Street

MON–FRI. 8:00am – 7:00pm
SAT. 10:00am – 6:00pm
SUN. Closed

First opened 2010
Roaster TAP Coffee
Machine Nuova Simonelli Aurelia II T3, 3 groups
Grinder Mazzer Robur E, Mazzer Kony E, Mazzer Super Jolly E, Mahlkönig Tanzania

Espresso £2.20
Cappuccino £2.60
Latte £2.60
Flat white £2.60

MAP REF.

16

TAP Coffee Tottenham Court Road

114 Tottenham Court Road, W1T 5AH

TAP's unbranded facade sets it apart on chain-dominated Tottenham Court Road. Look closer and you'll notice a vintage bicycle suspended above the doorway; a motif which also graces the takeaway cups and ingeniously illustrated loyalty cards. The interior fuses exposed light bulbs, copper piping and white ceramic that recalls London's Victorian heyday. The attention to detail displayed towards the design is also evident in the coffee preparation. The baristas use separate blends for espresso and milk coffees, and single origin beans can be sampled on filter.

+44(0)20 7580 2163
www.tapcoffee.co.uk
 Warren Street

Sister locations Rathbone Place / Wardour Street

MON–FRI. 8:00am – 7:00pm
SAT. 10:00am – 6:00pm
SUN. Closed

First opened 2011
Roaster TAP Coffee
Machine Nuova Simonelli Aurelia Competizione, 3 groups
Grinder Mazzer Robur E, Mazzer Kony E, Mazzer Super Jolly E, Mahlkönig Tanzania

Espresso £2.20
Cappuccino £2.70
Latte £2.70
Flat white £2.70

MAP REF. 18

COFFEE 4.50 / 5

OVERALL 4.50 / 5 ★★★★✬

Taylor St Baristas Mayfair

22 Brooks Mews, W1K 4DY

Photo courtesy of the venue

Hidden away down a little mews, this small café is popular with suited up professionals. The sunlit interior features dark antique furniture, a slate floor and reclaimed church pews. The Taylor St independent chain has built its reputation on consistently excellent coffee, but just as importantly, well-trained and friendly staff. This is especially true at the Mayfair store, where baristas and customers banter freely with one another, and has led to the creation of the competitive 'Super frequent coffee freaks' loyalty blackboard.

+44(0)20 7629 3163
www.taylor-st.com
⊖ Bond Street

Sister locations Liverpool Street / Shoreditch / Canary Wharf / Monument / Bank / South Quay

MON-FRI. 7:30am - 5:30pm
SAT-SUN. Closed

First opened 2011
Roaster Union Hand-Roasted and guests
Machine La Marzocco Linea, 3 groups
Grinder Mazzer Kony E, Mazzer Super Jolly, Anfim

Espresso £2.00
Cappuccino £2.80 / £3.20
Latte £2.80 / £3.20
Flat white £2.80 / £3.70

MAP REF. **19**

COFFEE 4.50 / 5		OVERALL 4.50 / 5	

Timberyard Seven Dials

7 Upper St Martin's Lane, WC2H 9DL

Timberyard's second outpost replicates the winning formula of the original Clerkenwell store. Split over two floors, the comfortable seating area downstairs is perfect for working away with a laptop, and two dedicated rooms are available to hire for business meetings or other gatherings. Customers can try the excellent Has Bean coffee brewed by Chemex as well as espresso, and the stellar tea service also deserves a special mention. Each teapot is served with a timer to ensure optimal brew time.

www.tyuk.com
Leicester Square / Covent Garden

Sister locations Clerkenwell

MON-FRI. 8:00am - 8:00pm
SAT. 10:00am - 8:00pm
SUN. 10:00am - 8:00pm

First opened 2014
Roaster Has Bean
Machine La Marzocco FB/80, 3 groups
Grinder Anfim, Nuova Simonelli Mythos, Mahlkönig Tanzania

Espresso £2.20
Cappuccino £2.80
Latte £2.80
Flat white £2.70

MAP REF. **20**

COFFEE 4.50 / 5	OVERALL 4.50 / 5
🫘🫘🫘🫘🫘	★★★★⯨

Workshop Coffee Co. Fitzrovia

80a Mortimer Street, W1W 7FE

Workshop Fitzrovia harks back to London's imperial zenith; its intricate tiling and gold details invoke Victorian grandeur. And then there's that bar: a sovereign slab of Madagascan granite, imbued with a magnetism which demands your gaze and touch. The coffee is precisely what you'd expect from Workshop: light-roasted and delicious. The baristas are efficient and deliberate, engaging customers with utmost politeness. There's a sense of mastery about the place; an irrefutable statement that in speciality coffee, London is enjoying a new heyday with Workshop at the vanguard.

www.workshopcoffee.com
⊖ Oxford Circus

Sister locations Marylebone / Clerkenwell / Holborn

MON-FRI. 7:00am - 7:00pm
SAT-SUN. 9:00am - 6:00pm

First opened 2014
Roaster Workshop Coffee Co.
Machine La Marzocco Linea PB, 3 groups
Grinder Mazzer Robur E x2, Mazzer Major E, Mahlkönig EK 43

Espresso £2.40
Cappuccino £3.00
Latte £3.20
Flat white £3.00

MAP REF. 21

COFFEE 4.75 / 5

OVERALL 4.75 / 5

Workshop Coffee Co. Marylebone

1 Barrett Street, W1U 1AX

At this smaller outpost of Workshop Coffee Co., coffee is a science and its baristas are laureates of the highest order. This is coffee at its best, brewed with clinical precision and minute attention to detail. Re-locating here from the former premises on Wigmore Street, Workshop's Marylebone outpost is the blueprint for a new kind of coffee bar. Simple bench seating runs the length of two walls and a small selection of pastries is enshrined behind polished glass. A range of Workshop's own beans and coffee-making equipment is available to buy.

www.workshopcoffee.com
⊖ Bond Street

Sister locations Clerkenwell / Holborn / Fitzrovia

MON-FRI. 7:00am - 7:00pm
SAT-SUN. 9:00am - 6:00pm

First opened 2015
Roaster Workshop Coffee Co.
Machine Synesso Hydra, 3 groups
Grinder Mazzer Robur E x2, Mazzer Major E, Mahlkönig Tanzania, Mahlkönig EK 43

Espresso £2.40
Cappuccino £3.00
Latte £3.20
Flat white £3.00

MAP REF. 22

COFFEE 4.75 / 5	OVERALL 4.50 / 5
🫘🫘🫘🫘🫘	★★★★⯪

For coconut and coffee lovers

Ask for the Alpro choice in your favourite coffee bar.
If you are a barista looking for new, check out the
'For Professionals' range, ingredients designed for you.
Visit Alpro.com/foodservice

enjoy plant power
alpro®

Soho

Famous for its outrageous nightlife, Soho is also well-known for its cutting-edge bars, clubs and restaurants. This spirit of experimentation and adventure extends to coffee and many of London's most exciting artisanal cafés can be found here.

Department of Coffee and Social Affairs

Carnaby Street 3 Lowndes Court, W1F 7HD

Photo courtesy of the venue

Occupying a light, modern space just off Carnaby Street, this branch of Department (formerly known as Speakeasy) is home to some of London's most talented baristas. The café offers an impressive choice of coffee beans: two espresso roasts complemented by two different single origins on filter. There's more to this stylish coffee bar than meets the eye, Department encourages a hands-on approach to coffee making, operating a coffee school in their dedicated downstairs space.

www.departmentofcoffee.com
⊖ Oxford Circus

Sister locations Norton Folgate / Leather Lane / Chancery Lane / Piccadilly / Covent Garden

MON-WED. 8:00am - 7:00pm
THU-FRI. 8:00am - 8:30pm
SAT. 10:00am - 8:30pm
SUN. 10:00am - 6:00pm

First opened 2011
Roaster Department of Coffee and Social Affairs
Machine La Marzocco FB/80, 3 groups
Grinder Mazzer Robur E x2, Mazzer Super Jolly, Mahlkönig Tanzania

Espresso £2.40
Cappuccino £2.90
Latte £2.90
Flat white £2.70

MAP REF. **23**

COFFEE 4.50 / 5

OVERALL 4.50 / 5 ★★★★⯪

Department of Coffee and Social Affairs
Piccadilly 15 Sherwood Street, W1F 7ED

This compact venue (formerly named Tonic) is a modern and sophisticated take on the traditional Italian espresso bar. Department is ideal for picking up an expertly-made brew before dashing to your next Soho appointment, but owing to the small space, it's not the best place to spread out with the broadsheets. Alongside Department's new house-roasted espresso blend, coffee aficionados will delight in the rotating range of single origin coffees brewed by Filtro Shuttle.

www.departmentofcoffee.com
 Piccadilly Circus

Sister locations Norton Folgate / Leather Lane / Chancery Lane / Carnaby Street / Covent Garden

MON-FRI. 7:30am - 5:30pm
SAT-SUN. 9:30am - 5:30pm

First opened 2013
Roaster Department of Coffee and Social Affairs
Machine La Marzocco FB/80, 2 groups
Grinder Mazzer Robur E x2, Mazzer Super Jolly, Mahlkönig Vario

Espresso £2.40
Cappuccino £2.90
Latte £2.90
Flat white £2.70

MAP REF. **24**

COFFEE 4.25 / 5		OVERALL 4.25 / 5	★★★★⯪

Fernandez & Wells Beak Street
73 Beak Street, W1F 9SR

This venue perfects Fernandez & Wells' signature combination of artisanal European food with superb coffee. Fernandez & Wells was one of the first coffee bars in London to install the high-end Synesso Cyncra espresso machine. This café retains its simple focus on fine coffee and food. The clean interior accentuates this priority with unadorned cream walls and rustic timber benches. Fernandez & Wells retains its position as a premier London coffee and foodie destination.

+44(0)20 7287 8124
www.fernandezandwells.com
 Piccadilly Circus / Oxford Circus

Sister locations Lexington Street / South Kensington / Somerset House / Denmark Street / Duke Street

MON-FRI. 7:30am - 6:00pm
SAT-SUN. 9:00am - 6:00pm

First opened 2007
Roaster Has Bean bespoke blend
Machine Synesso Cyncra, 3 groups
Grinder Mazzer Robur E, Ditting

Espresso £2.40
Cappuccino £2.80
Latte £2.80
Flat white £2.80

MAP REF. **25**

COFFEE 4.25 / 5	OVERALL 4.50 / 5	★★★★⯪

Fernandez & Wells Denmark Street

1-3 Denmark Street, WC2H 8LP

One of the early proponents of speciality coffee in London, Fernandez & Wells is a food and drink emporium satisfying the most fervid foodie yearning. Do you have a hankering for ham? Try the Iberian cured meats from Brindisa. Are you partial to pressed juice? Freshly squeezed blood orange for you. When it comes to coffee, Jorge Fernandez is as experienced as they come, having managed Monmouth's Covent Garden store before most Londoners sipped their first flat white. The impressive new Denmark Street site is a temple to temptation which must be visited.

+44(0)20 3302 9799
www.fernandezandwells.com
⊖ Tottenham Court Road

Sister locations Beak Street / Lexington Street / Duke Street / South Kensington / Somerset House

MON-WED. 8:00am - 9:00pm
THU-FRI. 8:00am - 10:00pm
SAT. 9:00am - 7:30am
SUN. 9:00am - 6:00pm

First opened 2014
Roaster Has Bean
Machine La Marzocco Linea PB, 3 groups
Grinder Mazzer Robur x2, Ditting

Espresso £2.40
Cappuccino £2.80
Latte £2.80
Flat white £2.80

MAP REF.

 COFFEE 4.25 / 5   **OVERALL** 4.50 / 5

Flat White

17 Berwick Street, W1F 0PT

Established in 2005, Flat White was one of the first cafés to bring antipodean-style coffee to the UK. For a time it became a London coffee institution, celebrated as a pioneer of third wave coffee in the capital. The venue has changed hands several times since those heady days, but fortunately there's now a renewed focus on quality. The interior has been refreshed and customers can expect a range of beans from renowned Swedish roasters Drop Coffee, pulled through an impressive 4-group Synesso, affectionately dubbed "The Great White"

+44(0)20 7734 0370
www.flatwhitecafe.com
⊖ Oxford Circus / Tottenham Court Road

Sister locations Milkbar

MON-FRI. 8:00am - 7:00pm
SAT-SUN. 9:00am - 6:00pm

First opened 2005
Roaster Drop Coffee
Machine Synesso Hydra, 4 groups
Grinder Nuova Simonelli Mythos

Espresso £2.20
Cappuccino £2.80 / £3.30
Latte £2.80 / £3.30
Flat white £2.70

MAP REF.

COFFEE 4.50 / 5	OVERALL 4.50 / 5
🫘🫘🫘🫘🫘	★★★★⯪

Foxcroft & Ginger Soho

3 Berwick Street, W1F 0DR

Photo courtesy of the venue

This modern-rustic Soho coffee house is a key feature of the vibrant Berwick Street community. A heavy wooden door leads into an industrial space decorated with a mixture of concrete, tile, brick and exposed piping. The intimate downstairs area offers a welcome retreat. In addition to hearty brunches and small wine menu, Foxcroft & Ginger bake their own sourdough bread and serve up delicious pizzas Monday through to Saturday.

www.foxcroftandginger.co.uk
Piccadilly Circus / Oxford Circus

Sister locations Whitechapel

MON. 8:00am - 7:00pm
TUE-FRI. 8:00am - 10:00pm
SAT. 9:00am - 10:00pm
SUN. 9:00am - 7:00pm

First opened 2010
Roaster The Roasting Party
Machine Synesso Cyncra, 3 groups
Grinder Anfim, Mazzer Robur E

Espresso £2.00
Cappuccino £2.50
Latte £2.50
Flat white £2.50

MAP REF. 28

COFFEE 4.50 / 5

OVERALL 4.25 / 5 ★★★★⯪

Milkbar

3 Bateman Street, W1D 4AG

Milkbar emerged from beneath the wing of Flat White to become one of Soho's most popular brunch venues. It has grown into a mecca for Kiwis and Aussies longing for a taste of home, and a place of discovery for Londoners experiencing the third wave's daringly light roasts. After a period of transition, this much-loved antipodean café is returning to form. The baristas' disarming informality, together with the venue's youthful, grungy feel make it a popular hangout for Soho creatives.

+44(0)20 7287 4796

⊖ Tottenham Court Road / Leicester Square

Sister locations Flat White

MON-FRI. 8:00am - 5:30pm
SAT. 9:30am - 6:00pm
SUN. 10:00am - 6:00pm

First opened 2008
Roaster Drop Coffee
Machine La Marzocco FB/80, 3 groups
Grinder Mazzer Robur, Mazzer Super Jolly, Ditting, Nuova Simonelli Mythos

Espresso £2.40
Cappuccino £3.00
Latte £3.00
Flat white £2.80

MAP REF. **29**

| COFFEE 4.50 / 5 | 🫘🫘🫘🫘🫘 | OVERALL 4.25 / 5 | ★★★★⯪ |

Nude Espresso Soho

19 Soho Square, W1D 3QN

Nude Espresso's signature East blend coffee has arrived in Soho. The interior here is sleeker and more understated than Nude Hanbury Street, but the staff are just as passionate about delivering excellent coffee to their urbane Soho customers. A range of tasty breakfast, lunch and sweet foods are prepared fresh by Nude chefs in the open kitchen. A selection of coffee equipment is also available to purchase, and Nude runs home brewing workshops to help customers get the most from their gear.

+44(0)7712 899 336
www.nudeespresso.com
⊖ Tottenham Court Road

Sister locations Hanbury Street / Nude Espresso Roastery

MON-FRI. 7:30am - 5:00pm
SAT-SUN. Closed

First opened 2011
Roaster Nude Espresso
Machine La Marzocco FB/80 3 groups
Grinder Nuova Simonelli Mythos

Espresso £2.20
Cappuccino £2.80
Latte £2.80
Flat white £2.80

MAP REF. **30**

COFFEE 4.50 / 5 **OVERALL** 4.25 / 5 ★★★★⯪

Princi

135 Wardour Street, W1F 0UT

A buzzing, lively eatery, Princi is a perfect fit for Soho and is packed with hungry customers all hours of the day and night. One length of the venue is occupied by tantalising displays of croissants, tarts, cakes, pizza and salads all made on site. The elegant dining area consists of granite tables and a long metal bench against a water-feature wall, and the large window frontage is perfect for people-watching on this entertaining street.

+44(0)20 7478 8888
www.princi.co.uk
⊖ Piccadilly Circus / Oxford Circus / Tottenham Court Road

MON-SAT. 8:00am - 12:00am
SUN. 8:30am - 10:00pm

First opened 2008
Roaster Small Batch Coffee Company, Dark Woods
Machine Synesso Hydra, 3 groups
Grinder Nuova Simonelli Mythos

Espresso £1.80
Cappuccino £2.50
Latte £2.50
Flat white £2.50

MAP REF. **31**

COFFEE 3.75 / 5 **OVERALL** 4.25 / 5 ★★★★⯪

Rapha Cycle Club

85 Brewer Street, W1F 9ZN

The perfectionism Rapha applies to its cycling gear is readily apparent in its approach to coffee; the espresso here is extraordinarily good. Try a shot made with Alchemy beans, pulled through a customised Synesso Hydra. Bike locks are available for those arriving on two wheels, and the vintage Italian cycling memorabilia adds to the café's sense of energy and momentum. Coffee is no afterthought here; Rapha has established itself as a coffee destination in its own right.

+44(0)20 7494 9831
www.rapha.cc
🔴 Piccadilly Circus

MON-FRI. 7:30am - 8:00pm
SAT. 8:30am - 7:00pm
SUN. 10:00am - 6:00pm

First opened 2012
Roaster Alchemy and guests
Machine Synesso Hydra, 2 groups
Grinder Mazzer Kony E, Anfim, Mahlkönig Tanzania

Espresso £2.50
Cappuccino £3.00
Latte £3.00
Flat white £3.00

MAP REF. **32**

COFFEE 4.50 / 5   OVERALL 4.50 / 5 ★★★★⯪

Sacred Ganton Street

13 Ganton Street, W1F 9BL

Photo: Gary Handley

The Sacred empire extends across four London locations but this is where it all began back in 2005. Owner Tubbs Wanigasekera is a proud New Zealander and this shines through in the decor and relaxed atmosphere that characterises this busy café. While the main upstairs area has a pleasing openness that extends out into the bustle of Carnaby Street, couches in the mellow basement area offer a cosy refuge in which to sip a cup of the delicious new 'Auckland' espresso blend.

www.sacredcafe.com
⊖ Oxford Circus

Sister locations Covent Garden (Stanfords) / Highbury Studios / Westfield

MON–WED. 7:30am – 10:00pm
THU–SAT. 7:30am – 11:00pm
SUN. 10:00am – 9:00pm

First opened 2005
Roaster Sacred House Roast
Machine La Marzocco Linea, 3 groups
Grinder Anfim Super Caimano, Mazzer Super Jolly

Espresso £2.10
Cappuccino £2.90 / £3.10
Latte £2.90 / £3.10
Flat white £2.90 / £3.10

MAP REF. **33**

  COFFEE 4.25 / 5 OVERALL 4.50 / 5 ★★★★

Soho Grind

19 Beak Street, W1F 9RP

The Grind & Co. empire is on a mission to make coffee sexy, and in what better neighbourhood to do it in than Soho. The second store from entrepreneur David Abrahamovitch and Australian DJ Kaz James is an enticing coffee and cocktail den complete with sanguine lighting and bass soundtrack. Satisfy your coffee cravings with a seductive flat white, then descend the steps - beneath the neon sign promising 'French lessons given downstairs' - to the basement speakeasy for an espresso martini.

+44(0)20 7728 7073
www.sohogrind.com
⊖ Piccadilly Circus

Sister locations Shoreditch Grind / Holborn Grind / London Grind

MON-THU. 7:00am - 11:30pm
FRI. 7:00am - 12:00am
SAT. 9:00am - 12:00am
SUN. 9:00am - 8:00pm

First opened 2014
Roaster Small Batch Coffee Company bespoke blend
Machine La Marzocco Linea PB, 2 groups
Grinder Nuova Simonelli Mythos, La Marzocco Vulcano

Espresso £2.20
Cappuccino £2.70 / £3.00
Latte £2.70 / £3.00
Flat white £2.70

MAP REF. 34

COFFEE 4.50 / 5 · OVERALL 4.50 / 5 ★★★★⯨

TAP Coffee Wardour Street

193 Wardour Street, W1F 8ZF

Formerly known as Tapped & Packed, TAP Coffee's newest venue is an impressive statement in coffee bar design. Two rows of tables draw the eye towards the magnificent Probat roaster. Low-hung spotlights highlight the interior's bare wood and gleaming steel fixtures. TAP serves its excellent house-roasted 'Jack of Spades' blend, and single origins at the dedicated brew bar. Connoisseurs will also appreciate the green tea offered as a palate cleanser. Visitors can expect exceptionally high standards from one of London's most accomplished coffee destinations.

+44(0)20 7580 2163
www.tapcoffee.co.uk
⊖ Tottenham Court Road

Sister locations Rathbone Place / Tottenham Court Road

MON-FRI. 8:00am - 7:00pm
SAT. 10:00am - 6:00pm
SUN. 12:00pm - 6:00pm

First opened 2012
Roaster TAP Coffee
Machine Nuova Simonelli Aurelia T3, 3 groups
Grinder Mazzer Robur E, Mazzer Kony E, Mazzer Super Jolly E, Mahlkönig Tanzania

Espresso £2.20
Cappuccino £2.60
Latte £2.60
Flat white £2.60

MAP REF. **35**

 COFFEE 4.75 / 5 OVERALL 4.75 / 5  ★★★★

Holborn & Bloomsbury

Dotted with beautiful squares and grand architecture, Bloomsbury offers refined, contemplative surroundings to enjoy coffee. Home to thinkers for centuries, the neighbourhood is anchored by numerous academic institutions and the imposing British Museum, as well as boasting a wealth of literary connections. Busy Holborn to the south is frequented by lawyers and journalists, conducting business in and around the many cafés.

Continental Stores

54 Tavistock Place, WC1H 9RG

Continental Stores is a new venture from the owners of highly regarded Store Street Espresso. The lofty ceilings and white walls create an unhurried, contemplative environment in which to catch up on reading or meet friends. A mixed crowd of professionals, students and academics trade ideas and conversation against a backdrop of modern artworks. With plenty of experience behind them and an enviable equipment setup, the barista team ensure the Square Mile coffee is presented at its best.

⊖ Russell Square / King's Cross St Pancras

Sister locations Store Street Espresso

MON–FRI. 8:00am – 6:00pm
SAT. 9:00am – 5:00pm
SUN. 10:00am – 4:00pm

First opened 2014
Roaster Square Mile Coffee Roasters and guests
Machine Synesso Cyncra, 3 groups
Grinder Nuova Simonelli Mythos, Mahlkönig EK 43

Espresso £2.00 / £2.20
Cappuccino £2.60
Latte £2.60
Flat white £2.60

MAP REF. **36**

COFFEE 4.50 / 5   **OVERALL** 4.50 / 5 ★★★★✦

Department of Coffee and Social Affairs
Chancery Lane 90 Chancery Lane, WC2A 1DT

Formerly known as Chancery Coffee, this outpost of the Department of Coffee and Social Affairs has been rebranded in line with the mother shop on Leather Lane. The coffee shop's friendly baristas demonstrate meticulous attention to detail at the controls of their bright red La Marzocco FB/80. The magnificent copper counter forms the focal point in the small space. The coffee is made to a consistently excellent standard, but with seating limited to a narrow bench, we suggest having yours to go.

www.departmentofcoffee.com
⊖ Chancery Lane

Sister locations Norton Folgate / Leather Lane / Piccadilly / Carnaby Street / Covent Garden

MON–FRI. 7:30am – 5:00pm
SAT–SUN. Closed

First opened 2012
Roaster Department of Coffee and Social Affairs
Machine La Marzocco FB/80, 3 groups
Grinder Mazzer Robur E, Mazzer Super Jolly E

Espresso £2.40
Cappuccino £2.90
Latte £2.90
Flat white £2.70

MAP REF. **37**

COFFEE 4.25 / 5   **OVERALL** 4.25 / 5 ★★★★✦

The Espresso Room

31-35 Great Ormond Street, WC1N 3HZ

Despite The Espresso Room's pocket-sized proportions, the amiable baristas manage the queue with practiced ease, pulling shots on the Synesso Hydra with utmost precision. Owner Ben Townsend is a sage figure in the capital's coffee scene, and can also be found leading coffee courses at the London School of Coffee. This tiny espresso bar is widely considered one of London's very best, with a focus on coffee quality few others can match. Join the line of hospital staff, lawyers, and dapper Lamb's Conduit fashionistas to discover why.

+44(0)7760 714 883
www.theespressoroom.com
⊖ Russell Square

MON-FRI. 7:30am - 5:00pm
SAT-SUN. Closed

First opened 2009
Roaster Round Hill Roastery bespoke blend and guests
Machine Synesso Hydra, 2 groups
Grinder Mazzer Robur E, Mahlkönig EK 43

Espresso £1.80 / £2.20
Cappuccino £2.80 / £3.40
Latte £2.80 / £3.40
Flat white £2.80 / £3.40

MAP REF. **38**

COFFEE 4.75 / 5		OVERALL 4.25 / 5	
🫘🫘🫘🫘🫘		★★★★⯪	

FreeState Coffee

23 Southampton Row, WC1B 5HA

Raising the banner for third wave coffee in Holborn, FreeState's experienced baristas serve excellent coffee with a dose of American-style enthusiasm. Mismatched furniture and an old school gym bench add character to the sunny interior. Opened by the team behind New Row Coffee, the café builds on its coffee pedigree with a wider selection of Union roasts and guest beans. Customers with time to linger can opt for single estate filter coffee served at the dedicated brew bar.

+44(0)20 7998 1017
www.freestatecoffee.co.uk
⊖ Holborn

Sister locations New Row Coffee

MON-FRI. 7:00am - 7:00pm
SAT-SUN. 9:00am - 6:00pm

First opened 2013
Roaster Union Hand-Roasted and guests
Machine La Marzocco Strada EP, 3 groups
Grinder Mazzer Robur E, Mazzer Super Jolly x3

Espresso £2.00
Cappuccino £2.60 / £3.40
Latte £2.60 / £3.40
Flat white £2.50

MAP REF. 39

 COFFEE
4.50 / 5

 OVERALL
4.25 / 5

Holborn Grind

199 High Holborn, WC1V 7BD

 NEW

Grind is very much in the pink, opening two new venues in 2014 with a new London Bridge site planned for early 2015.

The company works with esteemed Brighton roaster Small Batch for its custom blend which is also the base of their famous espresso martinis, not to mention the hot flat white Russian. The bar's huge windows and corner location adjoining the newly-opened Hoxton Hotel affords customers the chance to see and be seen. Holborn Grind is helping to transform this previously transient neighbourhood into a vibrant food and drink destination.

+44(0)20 3693 3400
www.holborngrind.com
⊖ Holborn

Sister locations Shoreditch Grind / Soho Grind / London Grind

MON–THU. 7:00am – 11:30pm
FRI. 7:00am – 12:00am
SAT. 9:00am – 12:00am
SUN. 9:00am – 10:30pm

First opened 2014
Roaster Small Batch Coffee Company bespoke blend
Machine La Marzocco Linea PB, 3 groups
Grinder Nuova Simonelli Mythos x3, La Marzocco Vulcano

Espresso £2.20
Cappuccino £2.70 / £3.00
Latte £2.70 / £3.00
Flat white £2.70

MAP REF. **40**

COFFEE 4.50 / 5

OVERALL 4.50 / 5 ★★★★✬

Hubbard and Bell

199-206 High Holborn, WC1V 7BD

Hubbard and Bell is a café, bar and grill occupying a swathe of the open plan foyer of the Hoxton Hotel. This slick, midcentury-inspired space hums with activity as hotel guests mingle with fashionably dressed media workers. The talented barista team have a background at some of London's top cafés, ensuring that the standard of coffee preparation is consistently high. Hubbard and Bell demonstrates that with the right approach, top-notch coffee can be served in a modern, fast-paced hotel environment.

+44(0)20 7661 3030
www.hubbardandbell.com
⊖ Holborn

Sister locations Barber & Parlour

MON-FRI. 7:00am - 2:00am
SAT. 8:00am - 2:00am
SUN. 9:00am - 6:00pm

First opened 2014
Roaster Origin Coffee and guests
Machine La Marzocco Strada, 3 groups
Grinder Nuova Simonelli Mythos x2, Mahlkönig EK 43

Espresso £2.50
Cappuccino £2.80
Latte £2.80
Flat white £2.80

MAP REF. 41

COFFEE 4.50 / 5

OVERALL 4.50 / 5 ★★★★

Knockbox Coffee

29 Lambs Conduit Street, WC1N 3NG

With its array of outfitters, Lamb's Conduit Street is a destination for the dapper man about town. The road is also home to another well-pulled-together outfit in the shape of Knockbox Coffee. Turkish owner, Mete Dogrul, has a meticulous eye for detail, creating the furniture and fittings himself with plywood and copper. Occupying a sunny corner, the café is perfectly positioned for people-watching. Relax with a Workshop coffee whilst tucking into a hearty sandwich or a glorious Little Bread Pedlar pastry.

www.knockboxcoffee.com
⊖ Russell Square / Holborn

MON–FRI. 7:00am – 5:00pm
SAT. 8:00am – 5:00pm
SUN. Closed

First opened 2014
Roaster Workshop Coffee Co.
Machine Synesso Cyncra, 2 groups
Grinder Mazzer Major

Espresso £2.20
Cappuccino £2.60 / £2.90
Latte £2.60 / £2.90
Flat white £2.60

MAP REF. **42**

 | **COFFEE** 4.25 / 5 |  **OVERALL** 4.25 / 5 ★★★★☆

Workshop Coffee Co. Holborn TOP 30

60a Holborn Viaduct, EC1A 2FD

Workshop Holborn is a coffee bar for perfectionists. Its design can be summed up in just one word: uncompromising. The interior details look like they were agonised over during many long nights of planning. Even the two La Marzoccos, gleaming on the marble bar, have been stripped of their metal fins for a more streamlined appearance. The meticulously dosed coffee flows from immaculate portafilters into satisfyingly weighty porcelain cups. Workshop's exacting philosophy might not be to everybody's taste, but there's no question it has redefined what we've come to expect from a coffee bar.

www.workshopcoffee.com
⊖ Farringdon / Chancery Lane

Sister locations Marylebone / Fitzrovia / Clerkenwell

MON–FRI. 7:00am – 7:00pm
SAT–SUN. Closed

First opened 2014
Roaster Workshop Coffee Co.
Machine La Marzocco Linea PB, 3 groups and 2 groups
Grinder Mazzer Robur E x3, Mazzer Major, Mahlkönig EK 43 x2

Espresso £2.40
Cappuccino £3.00
Latte £3.20
Flat white £3.00

MAP REF. **43**

  **COFFEE** 4.75 / 5 |  **OVERALL** 4.75 / 5 ★★★★★

Farringdon & Clerkenwell

Formerly hubs of manufacturing and enterprise, the districts of Farringdon and Clerkenwell now house smart offices, loft apartments, night clubs and restaurants. Some of the most exciting coffee venues in town can also be found here, making this the new heart of London's burgeoning coffee culture.

Caravan Exmouth Market

11-13 Exmouth Market, EC1R 4QD

Photo: Gary Handley

Caravan roastery and restaurant is a popular fixture on the diverse Exmouth Market food and coffee scene. This modern dining venue is always busy, particularly on sunny days when patrons spill out onto the pavement, and plenty of options on the menu make this a popular destination for a weekend brunch or casual dinner. As well as espresso, a wide variety of coffee brewing methods are on offer, allowing patrons to appreciate the full range of flavours found in Caravan house roasts.

+44(0)20 7833 8115
www.caravanonexmouth.co.uk
⊖ Angel / Farringdon

Sister locations King's Cross

MON-WED. 8:00am - 11:00pm
THU-FRI. 8:00am - 12:00am
SAT. 10:00am - 12:00am
SUN. 10:00am - 10:30pm

First opened 2010
Roaster Caravan Coffee Roasters
Machine La Marzocco FB/80, 3 groups
Grinder Mazzer Robur E x2, Ditting KR 804, Mahlkönig K 30

Espresso £2.00
Cappuccino £2.60
Latte £2.60
Flat white £2.60

MAP REF. **44**

COFFEE 4.50 / 5 OVERALL 4.50 / 5 ★★★★⯪

Department of Coffee and Social Affairs

Leather Lane 14-16 Leather Lane, EC1N 7SU

Department of Coffee and Social Affairs is a key player on the booming Farringdon coffee scene. Occupying a former ironmonger's premises across two shopfronts, this generous space features an unpolished wood and exposed brick theme with plentiful seating. Department now roasts its own coffee in collaboration with Ben Presland, an expert coffee roaster known for roasting for the Tate and UK Barista Champion Maxwell Colonna-Dashwood.

+44(0)20 7419 6906
www.departmentofcoffee.co.uk
⊖ Chancery Lane / Farringdon

Sister locations Chancery Lane / Norton Folgate / Carnaby Street / Piccadilly / Covent Garden

MON-FRI. 7:00am - 6:00pm
SAT-SUN. 10:00am - 4:00pm

First opened 2010
Roaster Department of Coffee and Social Affairs
Machine La Marzocco FB/80, 3 groups
Grinder Mazzer Robur E x2, Mazzer Super Jolly

Espresso £2.40
Cappuccino £2.90
Latte £2.90
Flat white £2.70

MAP REF. 45

COFFEE 4.50 / 5	OVERALL 4.50 / 5
🫘🫘🫘🫘🫘	★★★★⯪

47

Fix

161 Whitecross Street, EC1Y 8JL

Discreetly occupying a former pub adjacent to the Whitecross St Market, Fix is a spacious and stylish place to drop in for a coffee and bite to eat. Fix serves a Climpson's blend custom-roasted to their exact specification. Big leather couches, well-chosen vintage furniture and quirky light fittings make this a comfortable and dynamic space in which to hang out. Creatives and visitors to the Whitecross Street market keep Fix buzzing on weekdays.

+44(0)20 7998 3878
www.fix-coffee.co.uk
⊖ Old Street / Barbican

Sister locations Fix 126

MON-FRI. 7:00am - 7:00pm
SAT. 8:00am - 7:00pm
SUN. 9:00am - 7:00pm

First opened 2009
Roaster Climpson & Sons bespoke blend
Machine La Marzocco Linea, 3 groups
Grinder Mazzer Robur E, Mazzer Super Jolly E

Espresso £1.60 / £2.00
Cappuccino £2.50 / £2.70
Latte £2.50 / £2.70
Flat white £2.50

MAP REF. **46**

COFFEE 4.25 / 5  **OVERALL** 4.25 / 5 ★★★★⯪

Ground Control

61 Amwell Street, EC1R 1UR

The Ethiopian Coffee Company's mission is to showcase the very best coffees from this unique part of Africa, including Yirgacheffe, Harrar and Sidamo. The company's Clerkenwell café, Ground Control, combines traditional Ethiopian curios with the sharp, space-age lines of a Kees van der Westen Mirage coffee machine. The company also retails beans at the Real Food Market behind the Southbank Centre (Fridays-Sundays) and Partridges Specialist Food Market in Chelsea (Saturdays).

+44(0)20 7502 1201
www.theethiopiancoffeecompany.co.uk
⊖ Angel

MON. 7:30am - 4:00pm
TUE-FRI. 7:30am - 5:00pm
SAT. 8:00am - 5:00pm
SUN. 9:00am - 4:00pm

First opened 2012
Roaster The Ethiopian Coffee Company
Machine Kees van der Westen Mirage, 2 groups
Grinder Anfim

Espresso £2.50
Cappuccino £2.90
Latte £2.90
Flat white £2.80

MAP REF. **47**

COFFEE 4.50 / 5  **OVERALL** 4.25 / 5 ★★★★⯪

Look Mum No Hands! Clerkenwell

49 Old Street, EC1V 9HX

Look Mum No Hands! has rapidly become one of the city's busiest destinations for those who love bikes and coffee in equal measure. This lively cafe and bike workshop is decorated with bicycles, bike parts, and vintage cycling memorabilia. A range of British craft beer is available on tap, and during the Tour de France, this place is a full-on party zone. The café hosts a range of bike-related events including cyclist speed dating nights. If you love bikes, coffee or both, Look Mum No Hands! is an essential destination.

+44(0)20 7253 1025
www.lookmumnohands.com
⊖ Old Street / Barbican

Sister locations Hackney

MON–FRI. 7:30am – 10:00pm
SAT. 9:00am – 10:00pm
SUN. 9:30am – 10:00pm

First opened 2010
Roaster Square Mile Coffee Roasters and guests
Machine Kees van der Westen Mirage, 2 groups
Grinder Anfim x2

Espresso £2.00
Cappuccino £2.80
Latte £2.80
Flat white £2.60

MAP REF. **48**

COFFEE 4.50 / 5	OVERALL 4.50 / 5
🫘🫘🫘🫘🫘	★★★★✭

Prufrock Coffee

23-25 Leather Lane, EC1N 7TE

Photo: Micha Theiner

Prufrock has achieved cult status in London, and international recognition for its progressive methods and tireless pursuit of coffee excellence. Founded by Gwilym Davies (2009 World Barista Champion) and Jeremy Challender, Prufrock is a premier destination to see unusual brew methods and sample rare coffees. The space also incorporates an SCAE accredited coffee training school catering to novices and barista champions alike. The extremely knowledgeable staff are enthusiastic about their craft, and welcoming to all.

+44(0)20 7242 0467
www.prufrockcoffee.com
⊖ Farringdon / Chancery Lane

MON-FRI. 8:00am - 6:00pm
SAT-SUN. 10:00am - 5:00pm

First opened 2011
Roaster Square Mile Coffee Roasters and guests
Machine Victoria Arduino Black Eagle, 3 groups
Grinder Mahlkönig Tanzania, Nuova Simonelli, Mythos x3

Espresso £2.20 / £2.60
Cappuccino £2.80 / £3.00
Latte £3.00
Flat white £2.80

MAP REF. **49**

COFFEE
5 / 5

OVERALL
4.75 / 5

Timberyard Clerkenwell

61-67 Old Street, EC1V 9HW

Neither rough-hewn nor rustic, as its name might suggest, Timberyard is a slick yet friendly operation with big ambitions. The large tables and comfy seating downstairs make the space perfect for work or business meetings. iPads pre-loaded with subscriptions to popular news sites are also available to use. Timberyard offers some excellent coffee options, including Has Bean's citrusy 'Jabberwocky' blend. Single estate coffees brewed by 2-cup Chemex are ideal to share with a coffee-loving friend.

+44(0)20 3217 2009
www.tyuk.com
Old Street / Barbican

Sister locations Seven Dials

MON-FRI. 8:00am - 8:00pm
SAT. 10:00am - 8:00pm
SUN. 10:00am - 6:00pm

First opened 2012
Roaster Has Bean
Machine La Marzocco FB/80, 3 groups
Grinder Anfim, Nuova Simonelli Mythos, Mahlkönig Tanzania

Espresso £2.20
Cappuccino £2.80
Latte £2.80
Flat white £2.70

MAP REF. **50**

COFFEE 4.50 / 5	OVERALL 4.50 / 5 ★★★★⯨

Workshop Coffee Co. Clerkenwell

27 Clerkenwell Road, EC1M 5RN

Workshop Coffee has experienced a meteoric rise. This temple to speciality coffee contains a café, restaurant and roastery, spanning multiple floors of an industrial themed space. A remarkable 'living wall' of plants adds a dash of green to the raw brick and steel. Attracting top talent from the UK, Australia and the US, Workshop is a young company with a reputation for roasting excellence. An array of single origins and popular 'Cult of Done' espresso blend are crafted on-site, and their coffee is now a frequent sight in some of the capital's finest coffee bars.

+44(0)20 7253 5754
www.workshopcoffee.com
⊖ Farringdon

Sister locations Marylebone / Holborn / Fitzrovia

MON. 7:30am - 6:00pm
TUE-FRI. 7:30am - 10:00pm
SAT-SUN. 8:00am - 6:00pm

First opened 2011
Roaster Workshop Coffee Co.
Machine La Marzocco Linea PB, 3 groups, La Marzocco Linea, 2 groups
Grinder Mazzer Robur E x3, Mazzer Major E x2, Mahlkönig Tanzania, Mahlkönig EK 43

Espresso £2.40
Cappuccino £3.00
Latte £3.20
Flat white £3.00

MAP REF. **51**

COFFEE 5 / 5	OVERALL 4.75 / 5

The City

London's centre of finance and commerce may not boast the sheer number of cafés as Soho or the West End, but several recent high-profile openings have rapidly transformed its coffee fortunes. The City is surprisingly quiet at weekends (and many coffee bars open Monday to Friday only), so the area is best experienced during the bustling work week.

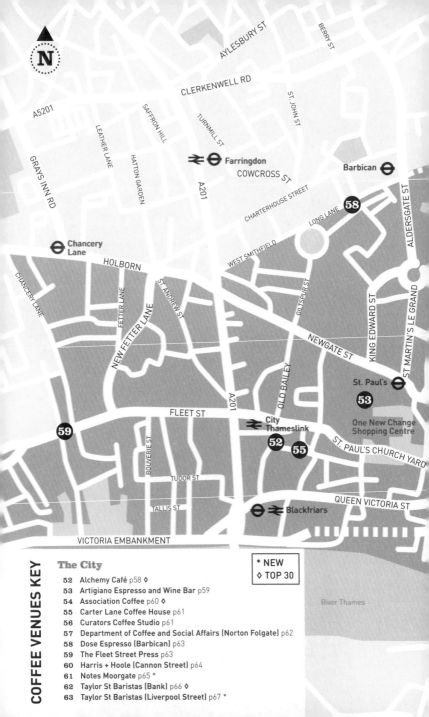

The City

* NEW
◊ TOP 30

COFFEE VENUES KEY

Alchemy Café

8 Ludgate Broadway, EC4V 6DU

TOP 30

The Alchemists of old attempted to transform ordinary materials into precious metals. This City café is well practiced in espresso alchemy; extracting liquid gold with an array of coffee apparatus, including a cold brew drip tower. The Alchemy wizards also operate a roastery in South London, which has earned a reputation as one of the capital's best up and coming roasters. Customers interested in delving deeper into the mysteries of espresso science can join one of Alchemy's coffee courses.

+44(0)20 7329 9904
www.alchemycoffee.co.uk
⊖ Blackfriars / ⇌ City Thameslink Rail

MON-FRI. 7:00am - 4:30pm
SAT-SUN. Closed

First opened 2013
Roaster Alchemy Coffee
Machine La Marzocco FB/80, 2 groups
Grinder Mazzer Robur E x2, Mazzer Mini, Mahlkönig EK 43

Espresso £2.00
Cappuccino £2.80
Latte £2.80
Flat white £2.60

MAP REF. **52**

 COFFEE 4.75 / 5   **OVERALL** 4.50 / 5

Artigiano Espresso and Wine Bar

1 Paternoster Square, EC4M 7DX

A dual-level coffee and wine bar near St Paul's Cathedral, Artigiano attracts City workers seeking more than just a habitual caffeine hit. Coffee is sourced from highly regarded Cornish roaster Origin Coffee, and prepared by a well trained barista team on a pair of custom-painted Lineas. Exposed brickwork and a contrasting grey and yellow design scheme create a striking backdrop. Go for lunch and you'll be hard pressed to resist the sandwiches, freshly prepared on-site with artisan bread.

+44(0)20 7248 0407
www.artigiano.uk.com
⊖ St Paul's

MON-TUE. 7:00am - 10:30pm
WED-FRI. 7:00am - 11:30pm
SAT-SUN. 10:30am - 6:00pm

First opened 2013
Roaster Origin Coffee bespoke blend
Machine La Marzocco Linea, 2 groups x2
Grinder Mazzer Major x2

Espresso £2.00
Cappuccino £2.70
Latte £2.70
Flat white £2.70

MAP REF. **53**

 COFFEE 4.25 / 5 🫘🫘🫘🫘🫘 **OVERALL** 4.50 / 5 ★★★★✬

Association Coffee

10-12 Creechurch Lane, EC3A 5AY

Association brings gourmet coffee and quality food from small suppliers to the heart of the City. A meticulously prepared range of pastries, cakes and sandwiches are served in sleek, yet accessible surroundings. The interior follows a familiar industrial template, but adds City-influenced twists including a tiled communal table studded with banker's lamps, offering a great spot for meetings or casual lunches. Association's brew bar should not be missed, manned by professional baristas who are serious about their craft.

+44(0)20 7283 1155
www.associationcoffee.com
⊖ Aldgate / Liverpool Street

MON-FRI. 7:30am - 5:00pm
SAT-SUN. Closed

First opened 2012
Roaster Square Mile Coffee Roasters, Workshop Coffee Co. and guests
Machine Synesso Hydra, 3 groups
Grinder Mazzer Robur E, Mazzer Kony E, Mahlkönig Tanzania, Anfim Super Caimano

Espresso £2.20
Cappuccino £2.80
Latte £2.80
Flat white £2.80

MAP REF. **54**

COFFEE 4.75 / 5   OVERALL 4.75 / 5

Carter Lane Coffee House

50 Carter Lane, EC4V 5EA

Nestled in one of London's narrowest streets, this pint-sized coffee bar means business. Sitting proudly on the immaculate counter is a high end Synesso Hydra, operated by well-trained Italian baristas. A small selection of pastries and toasted sandwiches complement the coffee. The space may be small, but the lively staff create a convivial atmosphere in which to escape the city throng. Carter Lane successfully blends East End coffee expertise with a clean-cut style sharper than a city boy's lapels.

+44(0)20 7248 9493
www.carterlane-coffee.co.uk
St Paul's / City Thameslink Rail

MON-FRI. 7:30am - 4:00pm
SAT-SUN. Closed

First opened 2012
Roaster Climpson & Sons
Machine Synesso Hydra, 2 groups
Grinder Mazzer Robur, Mazzer Mini

Espresso £1.50 / £1.80
Cappuccino £2.50 / £2.90
Latte £2.50 / £2.90
Flat white £2.40

MAP REF. **55**

 COFFEE 4.25 / 5  | OVERALL 4.25 / 5 ★★★★✩

Curators Coffee Studio

9a Cullum Street, EC3M 7JJ

There's a fine line between coffee and art at this small City café from former Kaffeine barista Catherine Seay. The vibrant turquoise La Marzocco Strada and matching grinders contrast with reclaimed wooden furniture and a vintage filing cabinet. Curators head barista and artist, Tim Shaw, illustrates selected takeaway cups. The superb coffee is accompanied by irresistible cakes from Bittersweet Bakers and pastries from Yeast Bakery.

+44(0)20 7283 4642
www.curatorscoffee.com
Monument / Bank

Sister locations Curators Coffee Gallery

MON-FRI. 7:30am - 5:30pm
SAT-SUN. Closed

First opened 2012
Roaster Nude Espresso, Square Mile Coffee Roasters
Machine La Marzocco Strada, 3 groups
Grinder Mazzer Robur E, Mazzer Mini, Anfim

Espresso £2.20
Cappuccino £2.80
Latte £2.80
Flat white £2.80

MAP REF. **56**

 COFFEE 4.50 / 5  | OVERALL 4.50 / 5 ★★★★✩

Department of Coffee and Social Affairs
Norton Folgate 201 Bishopgate, Norton Folgate, EC2M 3UG

Norton Folgate was a tiny self-governing area of East London that spanned just a few blocks up until 1855 and still gives its name to a short stretch of the A10. This narrow, sun-filled venue features a takeaway zone at one end and an eat-in area at the other. Custom-made lights inspired by the molecular structure of caffeine combine with a minimal black-and-white decor, high ceilings and huge windows to create a serene, crystalline space.

www.departmentofcoffee.com
Liverpool Street / Shoreditch High Street

Sister locations Leather Lane / Chancery Lane / Carnaby Street / Piccadilly / Covent Garden

MON-FRI. 7:00am - 5:30pm
SAT-SUN. 10:00am - 4:00pm

First opened 2012
Roaster Department of Coffee and Social Affairs
Machine La Marzocco FB/80, 3 groups
Grinder Mazzer Robur E x2, Mazzer Super Jolly, Mahlkönig Tanzania

Espresso £2.40
Cappuccino £2.90
Latte £2.90
Flat white £2.70

MAP REF. 57

COFFEE
4.25 / 5

OVERALL
4.25 / 5
★ ★ ★ ★ ☆

Dose Espresso Barbican

70 Long Lane, EC1A 9EJ

Straddling the border between the City and Farringdon, Dose Espresso is recognised as a leader in London's artisanal coffee scene. Owner and barista James Phillips sets a high standard in his small but welcoming espresso bar. All Dose coffee, milk and ingredients are ethically sourced and environmental consciousness is an important part of the company's identity.

+44(0)20 7600 0382
www.dose-espresso.com
⊖ Barbican

Sister locations Whitechapel

MON-FRI. 7:00am - 5:00pm
SAT. 9:00am - 4:00pm
SUN. Closed

First opened 2009
Roaster Square Mile Coffee Roasters and guests
Machine Synesso Hydra, 3 groups
Grinder Ceado E92, Anfim Super Caimano, Mahlkönig Tanzania

Espresso £2.00 / £2.20
Cappuccino £2.80 / £3.20
Latte £2.80 / £3.20
Flat white £2.80 / £3.20   MAP REF. **58**

COFFEE 4.50 / 5    **OVERALL** 4.50 / 5   ★★★★⯪

The Fleet Street Press

3 Fleet Street, EC4Y 1AU

The Fleet Street Press occupies a listed building complete with stunning stained glass window, and serves a mixed crowd of lawyers and students. Owners Davide Pastorino and Andy Wells oversee a friendly team pulling shots of Caravan coffee on a brand new La Marzocco. Expect top notch suppliers including non-homogenised milk from the Goodwood Dairy, and a healthy dose of witticisms dispensed to passers-by on what is surely London's most amusing pavement A-board sign.

+44(0)20 7583 7757
⊖ Temple

MON-FRI. 6:30am - 6:30pm
SAT-SUN. 10:00am - 5:00pm

First opened 2011
Roaster Caravan and guests
Machine La Marzocco GB/5, 3 groups
Grinder La Marzocco Vulcano, Mazzer Mini, Mahlkönig Tanzania

Espresso £2.00
Cappuccino £2.30 / £2.60
Latte £2.30 / £2.60
Flat white £2.50

MAP REF. **59**

COFFEE 4.25 / 5    **OVERALL** 4.00 / 5   ★★★★☆

Harris + Hoole Cannon Street

113 Cannon Street, EC4N 5AW

Named after two coffee loving characters in the diaries of Samuel Pepys, Harris + Hoole is a new breed of coffee bar bringing artisan-style coffee to the high street. Founded by the Tolley siblings (owners of Taylor St Baristas), Harris + Hoole draws on a high level of coffee expertise and quality suppliers. This impressive flagship store is busy, yet runs efficiently thanks to well-trained staff and a digital ordering system. The company is set to replicate this success throughout the rest of the UK with an ambitious expansion programme.

+44(0)20 7621 0526
www.harrisandhoole.co.uk
Cannon Street / Bank

Sister locations Central London: Tooley Street / London Wall / King's Cross

MON-FRI. 6:30am - 7:00pm
SAT. 10:00am - 4:00pm
SUN. Closed

First opened 2013
Roaster Union Hand-Roasted
Machine Nuova Simonelli Aurelia II T3, 3 groups x3
Grinder Nuova Simonelli Mythos x6

Espresso £1.95
Cappuccino £2.30 / £2.60 / £3.00
Latte £2.30 / £2.60 / £3.00
Flat white £2.30 / £2.90 / £3.50

MAP REF. 60

 COFFEE 4.25 / 5   **OVERALL** 4.50 / 5 ★★★★⯨

Notes Moorgate

CityPoint, 1 Ropemaker Street, EC2Y 9AW

Notes Moorgate suits drinkers whose coffee habit gradually transforms into a wine habit as day turns to night. When the coffee menu and wine list are as dependable as they are here, it's a habit to strive for if you ask us. The crescent-shaped space on the ground floor of the towering CityPoint building creates a breathtaking architectural backdrop to the sensory experience within. Notes has earned a hard-won reputation for sourcing and roasting excellent coffee, and its first City location is the ideal setting to enjoy the fruits of the roaster's labour.

+44(0)20 7628 5175
www.notes-uk.co.uk
⊖ Moorgate

Sister locations Trafalgar Square / Canary Wharf / Kings Cross

MON-TUE. 7:00am - 9:00pm
WED-FRI. 7:00am - 10:00pm
SAT-SUN. Closed

First opened 2014
Roaster Notes Coffee Roasters
Machine La Marzocco Linea PB, 2 groups x2
Grinder Nuova Simonelli Mythos x2,
Mahlkönig EK 43

Espresso £2.00 / £2.40
Cappuccino £2.80
Latte £2.80
Flat white £2.80

MAP REF. **61**

COFFEE 4.50 / 5	OVERALL 4.50 / 5

Taylor St Baristas Bank

125 Old Broad Street, EC2N 1AR

Photo courtesy of the venue

The Bank venue is one of the largest and busiest cafés in the Taylor St Baristas family. The sleek and spacious design includes lofty ceilings, timber finishing and designer drop lights. There's plenty of seating, making this a great place for a business meeting or lunchtime escape. Scrumptious lunch options are also on offer. The guest espresso changes every fortnight, and seasonal single origin coffees are served at the dedicated brew bar.

+44(0)20 7256 8665
www.taylor-st.com
⊖ Bank / Liverpool Street

Sister locations Liverpool Street / Shoreditch / Canary Wharf / Monument / Mayfair / South Quay

MON-FRI. 7:00am - 6:00pm
SAT-SUN. Closed

First opened 2010
Roaster Union Hand-Roasted and guests
Machine Nuova Simonelli Aurelia II T3, 3 groups, x2, Nuova Simonelli Appia, 3 groups
Grinder Mazzer Robur E x3, Anfim x2, Ditting

Espresso £2.00
Cappuccino £2.80 / £3.20
Latte £2.80 / £3.20
Flat white £2.80 / £3.70

MAP REF. **62**

| COFFEE 4.50 / 5 | | OVERALL 4.50 / 5 | ★ ★ ★ ★ |

Taylor St Baristas Liverpool Street

1a New Street, EC2M 4TP

The atmosphere at the smallest Taylor St venue is thick with intoxicating coffee aromas layered with heavy bass from the oversized soundsystem. The morning rush swells the narrow space, steam rolls and grinders spin up as the crack team of baristas perform in perfect synchrony, deftly working the queue to a quickening tempo. This accelerated coffee bar is a slingshot for the City's office workers, propelling them towards offices, meetings and spreadsheets. It's a far cry from the larger Taylor St cafés, this store marches to an altogether different beat.

+44(0)20 7929 2207
www.taylor-st.com
⊖ Liverpool Street

Sister locations Bank / Shoreditch / Canary Wharf / Monument / Mayfair / South Quay

MON–FRI. 7:00am – 5:00pm
SAT–SUN. Closed

First opened 2008
Roaster Union Hand-Roasted and guests
Machine Nuova Simonelli Aurelia, 3 groups and 2 groups
Grinder Anfim x3, Mazzer Robur, Mahlkönig Tanzania

Espresso £2.00
Cappuccino £2.80 / £3.20
Latte £2.80 / £3.20
Flat white £2.80 / £3.70

MAP REF. **63**

COFFEE 4.50 / 5	OVERALL 4.00 / 5

North

The fashionable boroughs of North London contain a huge variety of venues, from the colourful cafés of Camden – the rock 'n' roll hub of yesteryear – to chic neighbourhood delis in Islington. Moneyed Hampstead retains an English village style charm, just a short tube ride away from central London. Home to both busy professionals and counter-culture figures, the area's coffee culture reflects North London's diversity and fascinating history.

The Bowery

47 Chalk Farm Road, NW1 8AJ

North

Camden has long been a destination for exhilarating music, but its coffee scene has lagged behind its sister neighbourhoods like a woebegone groupie. The Bowery (formerly named Tower 47) is on a mission to put Camden back in the limelight. The space incorporates a coffee bar, art gallery and event space. An ensemble of London's rockstar roasters grace the coffee menu, served with plenty of New York-style enthusiasm. The Bowery draws on a shared love of coffee, music and the electric energy of Camden's streets.

+44(0)20 7482 2274
www.bbbcamden.co.uk
⊖ Chalk Farm

MON-FRI. 7:30am - 5:00pm
SAT-SUN. 9:00am - 5:30pm

First opened 2013
Roaster Volcano Coffee Works, Alchemy and guests
Machine La Spaziale S40, 3 groups
Grinder Mazzer Major, Mazzer Super Jolly, Mazzer Mini E, Ditting

Espresso £1.90
Cappuccino £2.50 / £2.75
Latte £2.50 / £2.75
Flat white £2.50 / £2.75

MAP REF. **64**

COFFEE 4.25 / 5

OVERALL 4.25 / 5 ★ ★ ★ ★ ⯪

Campbell & Syme

9 Fortis Green, N2 9JR

East Finchley may not be fashionable territory for a roastery café, but don't let this make you underestimate Campbell & Syme. The business was established by Joe Syme, an experienced hand in the catering sector, Jon Cowell, a musician and long-time coffee aficionado, and Dumo Mathema, who learnt his roasting craft at Union. The team offer a variety of blends and single origins, and are working to secure direct relationships with individual producers, underlining their commitment to responsibly sourcing top quality coffee.

+44(0)7977 514 054
www.campbellandsyme.co.uk
⊖ East Finchley

MON–FRI. 7:30am – 2:00pm
SAT. 9:00am – 2:00pm
SUN. Closed

First opened 2012
Roaster Campbell & Syme
Machine La Marzocco GB/5, 3 groups
Grinder Mazzer Major, Anfim, Mahlkönig Tanzania

Espresso £2.00
Cappuccino £2.50
Latte £2.50
Flat white £2.50

MAP REF. **65**

COFFEE 4.50 / 5	OVERALL 4.25 / 5

Caravan King's Cross

1 Granary Square, N1C 4AA

Inhabiting a monolithic former granary building, Caravan has graduated to the major league in both London's coffee and casual dining arenas. The unabashed use of concrete and other reclaimed materials create an industrial atmosphere on a grand scale. The knowledgeable baristas are happy to offer advice on their seasonal blends, which are freshly roasted on the premises. The worldly food menu and wide range of coffees offer an excellent opportunity to experiment with coffee and food pairings.

+44(0)20 7101 7661
www.caravankingscross.co.uk
⊖ King's Cross St Pancras

Sister locations Exmouth Market

MON-FRI. 8:00am – 11:30pm
SAT. 10:00am – 11:30pm
SUN. 10:00am – 4:00pm

First opened 2012
Roaster Caravan Coffee Roasters
Machine La Marzocco Strada EP, 3 groups, La Marzocco Linea, 2 groups
Grinder Mazzer Robur E x4, Mahlkönig Tanzania

Espresso £2.00
Cappuccino £2.60
Latte £2.60
Flat white £2.60

MAP REF.

 **COFFEE** 4.75 / 5

 **OVERALL** 5 / 5 ★★★★★

Coffee Circus

136 Crouch Hill, N8 9DX

With its circus theme and vintage tearoom feel, Coffee Circus is a friendly, whimsical place to discover. The café's hidden location seemingly cultivates the eccentricity and playfulness hidden within, it wouldn't surprise us if it conceals a cupboard with a portal to a fantasy land. In addition to the well-poured coffee, expect a fanciful food menu including eggs and buttered soldiers. Coffee Circus transforms into an occasional evening performance space, but the curious visitor is more likely to stumble upon jazz nights than performing elephants. But we can always hope.

+44(0)20 8340 8221
www.coffeecircus.co.uk
⊖ Crouch Hill

MON-FRI. 8:00am – 6:00pm
SAT-SUN. 9:00am – 6:00pm

First opened 2010
Roaster Mission Coffee Works
Machine Nuova Simonelli Aurelia, 2 groups
Grinder Mazzer Major E, Anfim, Mahlkönig Vario, Ditting

Espresso £1.80
Cappuccino £2.50
Latte £2.50
Flat white £2.50

MAP REF. **67**

COFFEE 4.25 / 5	OVERALL 4.25 / 5
🫘🫘🫘🫘◗	★★★★✦

The Coffee Works Project

96-98 Islington High Street, N1 8EG

The Coffee Works Project owner Peter Theoklitou comes from a family of chefs and it shows. This stunning venue offers top-quality coffee and a fine deli menu. The centrepiece of the café is a beautiful Seattle-made Slayer espresso machine – the first of its kind in London. A variety of Has Bean seasonal roasts are available as espresso and on filter, complemented by a range of British cheeses and charcuterie. The Coffee Works Project is a fantastic addition to the London coffee scene and a must-visit destination.

+44(0)20 7424 5020
www.coffeeworksproject.com
⊖ Angel

MON–FRI. 7:30am - 6:00pm
SAT. 9:00am - 6:00pm
SUN. 10:00am - 5:00pm

First opened 2012
Roaster Has Bean
Machine Slayer, 3 groups
Grinder Nuova Simonelli Mythos, Anfim x2, Mahlkönig EK 43

Espresso £2.00
Cappuccino £2.80
Latte £2.80
Flat white £2.80

MAP REF. **68**

COFFEE 4.50 / 5

OVERALL 4.75 / 5

74

Drink, Shop & Dash

11 Caledonian Road, N1 9DX

For a small space predominantly serving takeaway, Drink, Shop & Dash offers an astonishing variety of beans and brew methods. In addition to espresso-based drinks, the visitor can order coffee brewed by V60, AeroPress, Chemex or even woodneck dripper. The enthusiastic baristas run Saturday cupping events, providing curious customers with the opportunity to learn more about flavour profiles and coffee theory. If time allows, it's worth browsing the quirky homewares at sister shop Drink, Shop & Do, located right next door.

+44(0)20 7278 4335
www.drinkshopdo.com
⊖ King's Cross St Pancras

Sister locations Drink, Shop & Do

MON-FRI. 7:00am – 5:00pm
SAT-SUN. Closed

First opened 2014
Roaster Alchemy
Machine Rocket Linea Professional, 3 groups
Grinder Anfim x2, Mahlkönig Tanzania

Espresso £2.00
Cappuccino £2.60
Latte £2.90
Flat white £2.40

MAP REF. **69**

COFFEE 4.25 / 5		OVERALL 4.25 / 5	

The Fields Beneath

52a Prince of Wales Road, NW5 3LN

Named after Gillian Tindall's 1977 historical study of Kentish Town, this small speciality coffee outpost has rallied a loyal local following. Owned by long-time coffee aficionado, Gavin Fernback, the converted railway arch at Kentish Town West station is a small but attractive coffee bar. Railway arches are often dark and rather foreboding sites, but nothing could be further from the truth here. The space is bathed in floods of light, illuminating the bare brick walls and the counter's intricate Moroccan-style tiling.

+44(0)7912 435 754
⊖ Kentish Town West

MON-SAT. 7:00am - 4:00pm
SUN. 9:00am - 5:00pm

First opened 2012
Roaster Tate Roasters and guests
Machine La Marzocco Linea, 2 groups
Grinder Nuova Simonelli Mythos

Espresso £2.00
Cappuccino £2.50
Latte £2.60
Flat white £2.50

MAP REF. **70**

COFFEE 4.50 / 5		OVERALL 4.25 / 5	

Ginger & White Belsize Park

2 England's Lane, NW3 4TG

Photo courtesy of the venue

Larger than its sister shop in Hampstead, Ginger & White Belsize Park was something of a happy accident - owners Tonia, Nicholas and Emma simply couldn't resist the high-ceilinged, sun-drenched corner venue when it became available. The café's kitchen supplies food to both Ginger & White stores. The large communal table is well-stocked with homemade peanut butter and preserves, while the cute upstairs area and outdoor tables are ideal spots to tuck into the moreish sandwiches and decadent cakes.

+44(0)20 7722 9944
www.gingerandwhite.com
⊖ Chalk Farm / Belsize Park

Sister locations Hampstead

MON-FRI. 7:30am - 4:30pm
SAT-SUN. 8:30am - 5:30pm

First opened 2012
Roaster Square Mile Coffee Roasters
Machine La Marzocco FB/80, 3 groups
Grinder Mazzer Robur E, Mazzer Mini

Espresso £2.20
Cappuccino £2.90
Latte £2.90
Flat white £2.90

MAP REF.

COFFEE 4.50 / 5	OVERALL 4.25 / 5
	★★★★⯪

Ginger & White Hampstead

4a-5a Perrin's Court, NW3 1QS

This proudly British café wears its heart on its sleeve. A local gem that is ever popular with the Hampstead community, Ginger & White serves well-crafted Square Mile coffee alongside modern British meals made using locally sourced produce. With the choice of a communal dining table, window seats or intimate leather sofas, this is a great place to enjoy a leisurely brunch.

+44(0)20 7431 9098
www.gingerandwhite.com
⊖ Hampstead

Sister locations Belsize Park

MON–FRI. 7:30am – 5:30pm
SAT–SUN. 8:30am – 5:30pm

First opened 2009
Roaster Square Mile Coffee Roasters
Machine La Marzocco FB/80, 3 groups
Grinder Anfim, Mazzer Robur E

Espresso £2.20
Cappuccino £2.90
Latte £2.90
Flat white £2.90

MAP REF. **72**

COFFEE 4.50 / 5	OVERALL 4.25 / 5

Lantana Camden

Camden Market, Camden Lock Place, NW1 8AF

After the success of Lantana Fitzrovia and Shoreditch, the Australian team opened their newest café in the heart of lively Camden Lock Market. Formerly named Ruby Dock, this café adds to the appeal of the area by bringing in specialty coffee and delicious small plates and cakes. It's an excellent place to catch a quick caffeine fix, rest weary feet and get some respite from the crowds. If you're in the mood for something stronger, the baristas will happily fix you a cocktail.

+44(0)20 7428 0421

⊖ Camden Town

Sister locations Fitzrovia / Shoreditch

MON–SUN. 9:00am – 5:00pm

First opened 2013
Roaster Alchemy bespoke blend
Machine La Marzocco Linea, 2 groups
Grinder Mazzer Robur E, Mazzer Super Jolly

Espresso £2.20
Cappuccino £2.70 / £2.90
Latte £2.70 / £2.90
Flat white £2.70

MAP REF. **73**

COFFEE 4.25 / 5 **OVERALL** 4.25 / 5 ★★★★☆

Leyas

20 Camden High Street, NW1 0JH

Camden High Street has long been the domain of coffee chain outlets, but this independent provides a welcome alternative. The spacious downstairs area is decorated with artwork and murals, and offers plenty of seating with mismatched tables and inviting chesterfield sofas. Leyas has upped the ante when it comes to coffee, offering up beans from Nude, Alchemy and Mission. This is also an excellent place to enjoy a leisurely brunch, served every day until noon, and until 3:30pm on weekends.

www.leyas.co.uk
⊖ Mornington Crescent

MON-FRI. 7:30am - 5:30pm
SAT-SUN. 9:00am - 6:00pm

First opened 2011
Roaster Rotating range including Nude, Alchemy and Mission Coffee Works
Machine La Marzocco GB/5, 2 groups
Grinder Mazzer Robur E, Mazzer Super Jolly x2

Espresso £2.00
Cappuccino £2.50 / £2.70
Latte £2.50 / £2.70
Flat white £2.50

MAP REF. **74**

COFFEE 4.25 / 5		OVERALL 4.25 / 5	★★★★⯪

Local Blend

587 Green Lanes, N8 0RG

Like an oasis in a desert of Turkish kebab houses and convenience stores, Local Blend finally brings speciality coffee to Harringay. The spacious Danish-inspired café feels like a living room, with comfy armchairs dotted around and a magazine stand overflowing with good reads. Owners Steve and Linda Talevski make you feel as though they are welcoming you into their own home. Climpson and Sons coffee, brunch and an array of sweet treats are served during the day, and a selection of wines, beers and cocktails are on offer in the evenings.

+44(0)20 8341 2939
www.localblend.co.uk
⊖ Turnpike Lane / Harringay Green Lanes

MON-FRI. 9:00am - 5:00pm
SAT-SUN. 10:00am - 5:00pm

First opened 2013
Roaster Climpson & Sons
Machine La Marzocco Linea, 3 groups
Grinder Mazzer Super Jolly, Mazzer Mini, Ditting

Espresso £1.90
Cappuccino £2.50
Latte £2.30
Flat white £2.30

MAP REF. **75**

COFFEE 4.00 / 5		OVERALL 4.25 / 5	★★★★⯪

Loft Coffee Company

4 Canfield Gardens, NW6 3BS

What Loft lacks in space, it compensates for with exceptionally friendly service, a welcome remedy to the scrum of Finchley Road. Sung-Jae Lee and his wife have created an uncomplicated, whitewashed space with warm wood panelling and a small number of tables. The Monmouth coffee is complemented by guest espresso such as Square Mile 'Red Brick'. Serving reliably excellent brews in an area not known for speciality coffee, Loft is a blessing for locals in search of a quality cup.

+44(0)20 7372 2008
⊖ Finchley Road

MON-FRI. 7:00am – 5:00pm
SAT. 8:00am – 4:00pm
SUN. 10:00am – 3:00pm

First opened 2012
Roaster Monmouth Coffee Company and guests
Machine La Marzocco Linea PB, 3 groups
Grinder Mazzer Kold

Espresso £2.20
Cappuccino £2.60
Latte £2.60
Flat white £2.60

MAP REF. **76**

COFFEE
4.25 / 5

OVERALL
4.00 / 5
★ ★ ★ ★ ☆

Maison d'Etre Coffee House

154 Canonbury Road, N1 2UP

This pretty café on the Highbury roundabout is a labour of love for owners Kim and Kostas, who gave up their day jobs to pursue a passion for food and coffee. Maison d'Etre serves a range of homemade cakes, sandwiches, treats and weekend brunch to an enthusiastic local crowd. Carefully selected suppliers include London Borough of Jam and Seven Seeded bakery. Hand-painted murals, vintage china and a welcoming atmosphere make this a serene spot to take five, particularly during the summer in the conservatory.

+44(0)20 7226 4711
www.maisondetrecafe.co.uk
⊖ Highbury & Islington

MON–FRI. 7:30am – 7:00pm
SAT–SUN. 9:00am – 6:00pm

First opened 2011
Roaster Square Mile Coffee Roasters
Machine La Marzocco Linea, 2 group
Grinder Mazzer Major, Mazzer Super Jolly

Espresso £2.00
Cappuccino £2.40
Latte £2.40
Flat white £2.40

MAP REF. **77**

COFFEE 4.00 / 5

OVERALL 4.00 / 5 ★★★★☆

81

Melrose and Morgan Primrose Hill

42 Gloucester Avenue, NW1 8JD

Photo courtesy of the venue

This grocer and deli in leafy Primrose Hill is a cornucopia of beautifully prepared, locally sourced food. Homemade preserves fill the shelves, alongside a daily selection of seasonal salads, sandwiches, soups and breads. Enjoy your coffee in the relaxing seating area while contemplating the irresistible range of cakes, tarts and tray bakes. Melrose and Morgan is one of London's very best purveyors of artisan produce, recognised with two 'Great Taste' awards.

+44(0)20 7722 0011
www.melroseandmorgan.com
⊖ Chalk Farm / Camden Town

Sister locations Hampstead

MON-FRI. 8:00am – 7:00pm
SAT. 8:00am – 6:00pm
SUN. 9:00am – 5:00pm

First opened 2004
Roaster Climpson & Sons
Machine La Marzocco Linea, 2 groups
Grinder Anfim

Espresso £1.70 / £1.95
Cappuccino £2.50
Latte £2.50
Flat white £2.50

MAP REF. **78**

 COFFEE 4.00 / 5   **OVERALL** 4.00 / 5 ★★★★☆

Saint Espresso

Angel House, 26 Pentonville Road, N1 9HJ

Saint Espresso says a lot about the status of coffee in London today. Aptly named due to its location in Angel House, Saint's interior is clean and understated. The elegant branding and subtle lighting creates a refined ambiance. The service is attentive and the baristas direct the attention of the curious customer towards tasting notes for the various beans on offer. If it wasn't for the espresso machine and retail display of coffee home brewing gear, this could just as easily be an upscale wine bar. Saint extols the virtues of the cult of espresso, and Londoners are converting in droves.

www.saintespresso.com
⊖ Angel

MON-FRI. 7:30am - 6:00pm
SAT-SUN. 9:00am - 6:00pm

First opened 2014
Roaster Rotating roasters
Machine La Marzocco Strada, 2 groups
Grinder Mazzer Robur, Mazzer Super Jolly, Baratza

Espresso £2.10
Cappuccino £2.70
Latte £2.70
Flat white £2.70

MAP REF. **79**

COFFEE 4.50 / 5	OVERALL 4.50 / 5
🫘🫘🫘🫘🫘	★★★★½

Sunday

169 Hemingford Road, N1 1DA

Sunday is the place you daydream about on a sullen Monday morning. Snuggled on a residential street in Barnsbury, this neighbourhood café's goal is to make every day feel like a weekend. It's a glowing composition of cappuccinos, broadsheets, broad smiles, pancakes and eggs. Molten yellow I've-made-it-to-the-weekend eggs. Pass through the doors and time slows down, because these Sunday hours are golden. Everything here comes together for beauty and good: the coffee is made with care and the brunch is unimpeachable. Sunday truly is a victory over the week gone by.

⊖ Caledonian Road & Barnsbury / Highbury & Islington

MON. Closed
TUE–WED. 8:30am – 6:00pm
THU–FRI. 8:30am – 10:30pm
SAT. 10:00am – 10:30pm
SUN. 10:00am – 5:00pm

First opened 2013
Roaster Caravan
Machine La Marzocco Linea, 2 groups
Grinder Mazzer Super Jolly

Espresso £2.00
Cappuccino £2.60 / £3.00
Latte £2.60 / £3.00
Flat white £2.60 / £3.00   MAP REF. **80**

| COFFEE 4.00 / 5 | OVERALL 4.25 / 5 ★★★★✩ |

Vagabond N4

Charter Court, Stroud Green Road, N4 3SG

Vagabond N4 brings top quality coffee to the otherwise sleepy Crouch Hill. The interior is artfully constructed with recycled wood and coffee sacks, while the coffee bar is manned by a team of extremely friendly and passionate baristas. In addition to espresso-based coffee, the café offers Sandows Cold Brew (Sandows operates its brewing operation in the basement of the Vagabond store on Holloway Road). A small number of tables outside offer the perfect spot to enjoy this refreshing caffeine beverage on a hot summer's day.

+44(0)75 2704 9414
www.vagabond.london
⊖ Finsbury Park / Crouch Hill

Sister locations Vagabond N7 / Vagabond E1

MON–SUN. 7:00am – 7:00pm

First opened 2012
Roaster Vagabond Coffee Roasters
Machine Nuova Simonelli Aurelia II, 3 groups
Grinder Mazzer Super Jolly, Ceado E37

Espresso £2.00
Cappuccino £2.30 / £2.50
Latte £2.30 / £2.50
Flat white £2.30 / £2.50

MAP REF. **81**

| COFFEE 4.50 / 5 | OVERALL 4.25 / 5 ★★★★✩ |

Vagabond N7

105 Holloway Road, N7 8LT

With their second venue, the Vagabond boys have perfected the deliberately unfinished interior look. The pockmarked walls and weathered wooden floorboards create a delightfully grungy vibe, and the enormous back room is home to an impressive new Giesen roaster. There's also an inviting, if somewhat ramshackle, rear garden.

The coffee is made with exceptional care, and single origins are available brewed by AeroPress or V60. Vagabond is an energetic, young coffee business with a roasting operation that promises to offer some excellent new coffees this year.

www.vagabond.london
⊖ Highbury & Islington

Sister locations Vagabond N4 / Vagabond E1

MON-FRI. 7:00am – 6:00pm
SAT-SUN. 9:00am – 6:00pm

First opened 2013
Roaster Vagabond Coffee Roasters
Machine Conti Monte Carlo, 2 groups
Grinder Mazzer Super Jolly, Ceado E37, Anfim, Mahlkönig EK 43

Espresso £2.00
Cappuccino £2.40 / £2.60
Latte £2.40 / £2.60
Flat white £2.40 / £2.60

MAP REF.

COFFEE 4.50 / 5	OVERALL 4.25 / 5
🫘🫘🫘🫘🫘	★★★★✦

Wired 194

194 Broadhurst Gardens, NW6 3AY

After a short stint on West End Lane, Wired has found a new home on nearby Broadhurst Gardens. Bare steel, reclaimed wood and industrial fittings create an austere first impression, but settle in with a brew and the atmosphere is soon enriched by the chocolaty notes of Climpson & Sons coffee. If sweet things are your weakness, you'll find plenty to tempt you, including lemon and poppy seed cakes from The Flour Station bakery. Thankfully for West Hampstead locals, this time around Wired looks set to stay.

⊖ West Hampstead

Sister locations Cable Co.

MON-FRI. 7:30am – 5:00pm
SAT-SUN. 9:00am – 5:00pm

First opened 2013
Roaster Climpson & Sons
Machine La Marzocco Linea, 2 groups
Grinder Mazzer Major, Mazzer Mini, Anfim

Espresso £2.00
Cappuccino £2.50
Latte £2.50
Flat white £2.40

MAP REF. **83**

 COFFEE 4.00 / 5   **OVERALL** 4.00 / 5

Carts & Kiosks

From neighbourhood farmers' markets to secluded city parks, London's coffee carts and kiosks caffeinate some of London's most captivating urban locations. Serving up coffee goodness in all weathers, these brave baristas are true heroes of the trade. Take the time to seek them out, and you'll soon discover a cadre of coffeeheads with fascinating stories to tell.

Bean About Town

Kentish Town Station, NW5 2AA

The distinctive green Bean About Town vans are a fixture on the streets of London, with six different outlets positioned at various points around town from Bow to Clapham. The Kentish Town outlet has been doing business since 2005 and is a trusted favourite with locals and commuters seeking a quality caffeine hit.

+44(0)20 3239 6432
www.beanabouttown.com
⊖ Kentish Town

Sister locations Kensington Olympia / Clapham North / Southbank / Bow Road Station

MON-FRI. 7:00am – 4:00pm
SAT-SUN. 9:00am – 4:00pm

First opened 2005
Roaster Richard Jansz
Machine Izzo Pompei Lever, 3 groups
Grinder Anfim

Espresso £1.60
Cappuccino £1.80 / £2.20 / £2.50
Latte £1.80 / £2.20 / £2.50
Flat white £1.80 / £2.20

MAP REF.

Blooming Good Coffee

Ezra Street, E2 7RH

Few places in London match Columbia Road market on Sundays for sheer sensory delight. The flower stalls are a riot of hues, the atmosphere alive with colourful market patter, and the air perfumed by hundreds of bobbing bouquets. Blooming Good Coffee adds the fruity notes of Square Mile espresso to the heady mix.

⊖ Hoxton

SUN. 8:00am – 2:00pm
MON-SAT. Closed

First opened 2002
Roaster Square Mile Coffee Roasters
Machine La Marzocco Linea, 3 groups
Grinder Anfim

Espresso £1.90
Cappuccino £2.40
Latte £2.40
Flat white £2.40

MAP REF.

Coleman Coffee

Dockley Road Industrial Estate, SE16 3SF

No trip to the artisan food producers of Spa Terminus is complete without a coffee from Coleman. Owner Jack has a refreshingly humble approach to his craft and a clear affinity with machinery, roasting beans with a restored 1950s Otto Swadlo roaster. The public can buy coffee and beans from the Saturdays-only stall located in Dockley Road Industrial Estate. Pull up a crate, order a cappuccino, and tuck into a pastry from neighbouring Little Bread Pedlar bakery.

+44(0)7809 496 695
www.colemancoffee.com
⊖ Bermondsey

SAT. 8:30am – 2:00pm
SUN-FRI. Closed

First opened 2011
Roaster Coleman Coffee
Machine La Marzocco Linea, 2 groups
Grinder 1970s Mazzer, Ditting

Espresso £1.50
Cappuccino £2.30
Latte £2.30
Flat white £2.30

MAP REF. **C**

Craft Coffee Cart

The Ropewalk, Maltby Street Market, SE1 3PA

Splintering away from touristy Borough Market, the thriving set of artisan traders at Maltby Street Market are passionate about their produce. Craft Coffee is no exception. The baristas are committed to coffee excellence, rain or shine. Dosing carefully and extracting with precision, their attention to detail puts many bricks and mortar cafés to shame. After the success of the cart, owners Emily and Jamie established their first permanent coffee shop in Shoreditch.

⊖ Bermondsey / London Bridge

Sister locations Shoreditch

SAT. 9:00am – 3:00pm
SUN. 11:00am – 4:00pm
MON-FRI. Closed

First opened 2012
Roaster Notes Roastery
Machine Nuova Simonelli Appia, 2 groups
Grinder Mazzer Robur E, Mahlkönig Tanzania

Espresso £2.00
Cappuccino £2.40
Latte £2.60
Flat white £2.40

MAP REF. **D**

Dark Fluid

Brockley Market, Lewisham College Car Park, Lewisham Way, SE4 1UT

South London locals flock to Dark Fluid's Brockley Market stall on Saturdays for coffee hand-roasted by passionate coffeehead Lawrence Sinclair. The growing number of local independent cafés now serving Dark Fluid coffee is testament to the microroaster's success. Brockley Market is a destination in itself, with artisan producers offering a smorgasbord of fine foods, from vegetables to charcuterie, accompanied by several stalls serving hot fare.

+44(0)7984 886 723
www.darkfluid.co.uk
⊖ Brockley / ⇌ St. John's Rail

SAT. 10:00am - 2:00pm
SUN-FRI. Closed

First opened 2011
Roaster Dark Fluid
Machine Custom-built lever machine, 3 groups
Grinder Mazzer Major

Espresso £1.50
Cappuccino £2.50
Latte £2.50
Flat white £2.50

MAP REF.

Espresso Base

St George's Churchyard, Bloomsbury Way, WC1A 2HR

Espresso Base nestles at the foot of St George's Bloomsbury, a magnificent church with English Baroque style architecture. The coffee cart is accompanied by a decking area with seating; the perfect spot for a sunny summer's day. Owner Gennaro is a charismatic Italian and coffee veteran with many years experience, and a story or two for those willing to listen. Himself a convert to third wave coffee, Gennaro's drinks are lovingly poured with finely textured milk and topped with beautiful latte art.

⊖ Holborn

MON-FRI. 8:30am - 4:30pm
SAT-SUN. Closed

First opened 2012
Roaster Has Bean
Machine La Marzocco FB/80, 2 groups
Grinder Mazzer Super Jolly, Mahlkönig Vario

Espresso £2.00
Cappuccino £2.50
Latte £2.50
Flat white £2.50

MAP REF.

Giddy Up

Fortune Street Park, EC1Y 0SB

Just around the corner from the famous Whitecross Street Market is Fortune Street Park, a charming patch of green in the backstreets of the Barbican that hosts one of the best coffee carts in London. Owner Lee Harte's barista street smarts were honed at the legendary Pitch 42, Columbia Road and Flat Cap coffee stalls. This expertise is evident in the attention to detail found here and at the sister carts.

Moorgate / Old Street

Sister locations Islington Memorial Green / Bep Haus / Newport Road Primary School

MON–FRI. 8:00am – 4:30pm
SAT–SUN. 10:00am – 4:00pm

First opened 2011
Roaster Square Mile Coffee Roasters, Has Bean
Machine La Marzocco GB/5, 3 groups
Grinder Anfim Super Caimano x2

Espresso £2.00
Cappuccino £2.60
Latte £2.60
Flat white £2.40

MAP REF.

Noble Espresso

Kings Cross Boulevard (at junction with Pancras Road), N1C 4T

There was a time when train station coffee conjured nightmarish images of dubious dark liquid in styrofoam cups. Thankfully those days are long gone. Commuters in North London can now pick up coffee expertly brewed by Shaun Young, former head barista at Kaffeine. Sited on Kings Boulevard outside redeveloped King's Cross station, the Noble Espresso cart is a saviour for red-eyed commuters. Part of the KERB street food collective, Noble Espresso is joined by other artisan food stalls trading Tuesday to Friday lunchtimes.

+44(0)7854 895 078
King's Cross St Pancras

MON–FRI. 7:00am – 3:00pm
SAT–SUN. Closed

First opened 2013
Roaster Rotating roasters
Machine La Marzocco Linea PB, 2 groups
Grinder Nuova Simonelli Mythos

Espresso £1.80 / £2.00
Cappuccino £2.50
Latte £2.50
Flat white £2.50

MAP REF.

Carts & Kiosks

Notes Coffee Barrows

60 St Giles High Street, WC2H 8LG

The polished wagons of Notes Coffee Barrows can be found dispensing fresh Notes espresso at three locations across London: in the churchyard of St Giles in the Fields; Duke of York Square, Chelsea; and among the artisan food traders of Borough Market (trading as Flat Cap Coffee in this location). The Notes carts are always a welcome sight around London and are synonymous with quality street coffee.

www.notes-uk.co.uk
Tottenham Court Road

Sister locations Borough Market / Duke of York Square

MON-FRI. 8:00am - 4:30pm
SAT-SUN. Closed

First opened 2009
Roaster Notes Roastery
Machine La Marzocco FB/80, 2 groups
Grinder Anfim

Espresso £1.60 / £2.00
Cappuccino £2.40 / £2.60
Latte £2.40 / £2.60
Flat white £2.40 / £2.60

MAP REF.

Terrone & Co.

Netil Market, 13-23 Westgate Street, E8 3RL

Located in Netil Market (near Broadway Market), Terrone is one of the few Italian third wave producers based in London. Originally from Salerno, enthusiastic owner Edy bucks the trend of the conservative Italian coffee fraternity with his lighter-roasted blends. The high standard of Terrone's coffee has already garnered plaudits, winning a gold star in the 2012 UK Great Taste Awards. Make the trip on a Saturday morning and wake up to an expertly poured Bianco Piatto (the Italian flat white).

www.terrone.co.uk
London Fields Rail

Sister locations Terrone at Pizza Pilgrims, Kingly Street

SAT. 10:30am - 5:30pm
SUN-FRI. Closed

First opened 2012
Roaster Terrone & Co.
Machine La Marzocco GB/5, 2 groups
Grinder La Marzocco Vulcano

Espresso £2.00
Cappuccino £2.70
Latte £2.70
Flat white £2.50

MAP REF.

Inner East

Brick Lane and Shoreditch provide London's creative pulse and are areas of tremendous diversity that have undergone rapid change in recent years. Many of the city's best new roasteries are based in East London and a range of artisan coffee venues provide fuel for the artists, students and urbanites who flock here for the weekend markets.

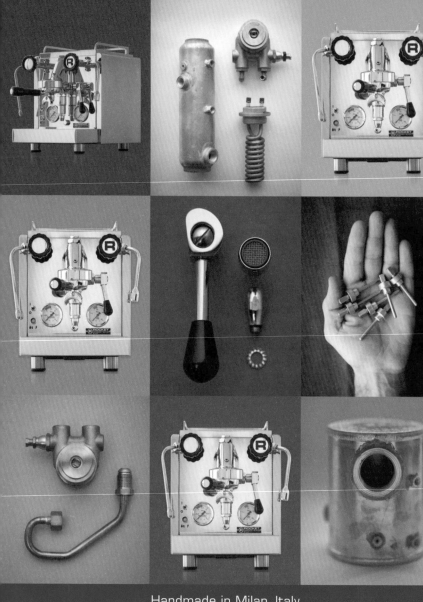

Handmade in Milan, Italy

OLD STREET
RIVINGTON ST
GREAT EASTERN STREET
SHOREDITCH HIGH ST
TABERNACLE STREET
SCRUTTON STREET
CURTAIN ROAD
WORSHIP STREET
CITY ROAD
WILSON STREET
PRIMROSE ST
BISHOPSGATE
ELDON STREET
FINSBURY CIRCUS
LONDON WALL
OLD BROAD ST
A10
HOUNDSDITCH
LIVERPOOL STREET
ARNOLD CIRCUS
CLUB ROW
SWANFIELD STREET
BETHNAL GREEN ROAD
COMMERCIAL STREET
QUAKER STREET
FOLGATE STREET
BUXTON STREET
SPITAL STREET
BRICK LANE
CHICKSAND STREET
OLD MONTAGUE STREET
COMMERCIAL STREET
WHITECHAPEL ROAD
ADLER STREET
ST. BOTOLPH ST
WHITECHAPEL ROAD
MINORIES
MANSELL ST
BROADCHURCH LANE
CHAMBER STREET
ROYAL MINT STREET
CARTWRIGHT STREET
A100

N

Street
Shoreditch High Street
Moorgate
Liverpool Street
Inner East
Aldgate East
Aldgate
Tower Gateway
Tower Hill
St Katharine Docks
River Thames

100 99 95 93 101 90 88 96 87 98 97 85 84 86 94 89 102 92 91 103

200   400m

Allpress Espresso Roastery

58 Redchurch Street, E2 7DP

This Kiwi roastery café is a firm favourite in the heart of Shoreditch. The café's simple, natural interior focuses attention on the coffee itself, and a gleaming roaster is proudly on display. Allpress has had huge success in New Zealand and Australia, and is continuing its winning run in the UK, supplying many high quality coffee shops and restaurants. In spring 2015 Allpress will open a brand new roastery café in a former joinery workshop in Dalston, an exciting new development for one of the country's top speciality roasters.

+44(0)20 7749 1780
www.allpressespresso.com
⊖ Shoreditch High Street

MON-FRI. 8:00am - 5:00pm
SAT-SUN. 9:00am - 5:00pm

First opened 2010
Roaster Allpress Espresso
Machine La Marzocco Linea PB, 3 groups
Grinder Mazzer Robur, Mazzer Super Jolly, Mahlkönig Tanzania

Espresso £2.00
Cappuccino £2.70
Latte £2.70
Flat white £2.70

MAP REF. **84**

 COFFEE 4.75 / 5

 OVERALL 4.50 / 5 ★★★★⯪

Barber & Parlour

64-66 Redchurch Street, E2 7DP

Barber and Parlour is a hybrid space on achingly hip Redchurch Street, catering for the East Londoner's every whim. The visitor will encounter a cinema, hair salon, nail bar and gentleman's barber before reaching the kitchen on the upper floor. Experienced barista, Petra, formerly of Taylor St, diligently oversees the coffee preparation. With excellent Origin beans in the hopper, the coffee aficionado has their caffeine fix sorted. The only choice that remains is: will you be following your espresso with a moustache trim or a Brazilian?

+44(0)20 3376 1777
www.barberandparlour.com
Shoreditch High Street

Sister locations Hubbard & Bell

MON-SAT. 9:00am - 10:00pm
SUN. 10:00am - 10:00pm

First opened 2014
Roaster Origin Coffee and guests
Machine La Marzocco Linea PB, 3 groups
Grinder Nuova Simonelli Mythos,
Mazzer Super Jolly

Espresso £2.50
Cappuccino £2.80
Latte £2.80
Flat white £2.50

MAP REF. **85**

COFFEE 4.25 / 5		OVERALL 4.50 / 5	

Brick Lane Coffee

157 Brick Lane, E1 6SB

Situated at the northern end of Brick Lane, the headquarters of the Street Coffee mini-chain oozes alternative cool. The mish-mash of vintage furniture, eclectic wall art featuring pop-culture icons and the bicycles crammed inside create a youthful, urban feel.

Art students and East London locals linger on the couches, except on Sundays when Brick Lane Market turns this café into a heaving hub for bargain hunters. The company's twitter provides a constant stream of irreverent entertainment, but is not for the faint-hearted.

+44(0)20 7729 2667
www.streetcoffee.co.uk
⊖ Shoreditch High Street

Sister locations Goswell Road / Bermondsey Street

MON-SUN. 7:00am - 8:00pm

First opened 2001
Roaster Dark Arts Coffee
Machine La Mazzocco Linea, 3 groups
Grinder Mazzer Kold, Mazzer Royal, Mazzer Robur

Espresso £1.60 / £1.70
Cappuccino £2.30 / £2.60 / £2.90
Latte £2.30 / £2.60 / £2.90
Flat white £2.40

MAP REF.

COFFEE 4.00 / 5   OVERALL 4.00 / 5

Brooklyn Coffee

139 Commercial Street, E1 6BJ

The interior design of Brooklyn Coffee will divide opinion. It's all clean lines, sharp corners and plate glass. The effect is multiplied by the monolithic concrete bar. Well-extracted Caravan coffee is made with precision by co-owner Bryan, who originally hails from New York City himself. Complement your flat white with a bar of artisan chocolate crafted by Williamsburg's achingly hip Mast Brothers. The store's interior may be austere, but the North American-style hospitality at Brooklyn Coffee is attentive and friendly.

www.brooklyncoffee.co.uk
⊖ Shoreditch High Street / Liverpool Street

MON-FRI. 7:00am - 5:00pm
SAT-SUN. 8:00am - 5:00pm

First opened 2014
Roaster Caravan
Machine La Marzocco Linea PB, 2 groups
Grinder Mazzer Robur, Mazzer Kony

Espresso £2.20
Cappuccino £2.80
Latte £3.00 / £3.20
Flat white £2.80

MAP REF. **87**

COFFEE 4.50 / 5	OVERALL 4.25 / 5 ★★★★⭐

Bulldog Edition at Ace Hotel

100 Shoreditch High Street, E1 6JQ

Bulldog Edition is a collaboration between Square Mile Coffee Roasters and hip hotel group, Ace Hotel. The coffee bar opens into the lobby, providing ample seating and first-rate people watching opportunities

Drawing on the roaster's expertise, Bulldog presents an innovative coffee menu, including 'filter shots', strong filter-style coffee extracted with the espresso machine at low pressure. The knowledgeable baristas run a smooth service with impeccable attention to detail, setting a new quality benchmark for hotel coffee.

+44(0)20 7613 9800
www.acehotel.com/london
⊖ Shoreditch High Street / Old Street

MON-SUN. 6:30am - 6:00pm

First opened 2013
Roaster Square Mile Coffee Roasters
Machine La Marzocco Strada, 3 groups
Grinder La Marzocco Vulcano,
Mahlkönig EK 43

Espresso £2.00 / £2.20
Cappuccino £2.60
Latte £3.00
Flat white £2.60

MAP REF. **88**

 COFFEE 4.75 / 5   OVERALL 4.50 / 5

Craft Coffee Shoreditch

68 Sclater Street, E1 6HR

Owners Emily Fahey and Jamie Evans have a wealth of experience in London's speciality coffee scene, including stints at Notes and running their Maltby Street cart. Their first bricks and mortar café retains the minimalist feel of the former art gallery, but adds a downstairs seating area for a cosy space to hide away with a book. Craft serves exceptional coffee in one of the capital's most competitive coffee neighbourhoods, and often offers some unusual guest beans.

www.craft-coffee.co.uk
⊖ Shoreditch High Street

Sister locations Maltby Street Market

MON–FRI. 8:00am – 5:00pm
SAT–SUN. 10:00am – 5:00pm

First opened 2013
Roaster Notes Roastery
Machine La Marzocco Linea, 2 groups
Grinder Mahlkönig EK 43, Ceado E92

Espresso £2.20
Cappuccino £2.80
Latte £2.80
Flat white £2.60

MAP REF. **89**

COFFEE 4.50 / 5	OVERALL 4.25 / 5 ★★★★⯪

Cream

31 New Inn Yard, EC2A 3EY

Howls of despair ricocheted through the Twittersphere in December 2014 when popular Shoreditch brunch spot Tuckshop announced it was vacating its premises. Fortunately, Magnus and the rest of the Tuckshop team have brought their innovative cooking to Cream, a new venture with in a converted warehouse just a few streets away. The Alchemy coffee is very well prepared, but the food deserves a special mention. Duck eggs, poached plum and caponata add fistfuls of flavour to the seasonal menu. When it comes to brunch, Cream definitely rises to the top.

+44(0)20 7247 3999
www.cream-shoreditch.com
⊖ Shoreditch High Street

MON-FRI. 8:00am - 4:00pm
SAT-SUN. 10:00am - 5:00pm

First opened 2015
Roaster Alchemy
Machine Kees van der Westen Mirage, 2 groups
Grinder Compak K-10 x2, Compak K-3

Espresso £2.00
Cappuccino £2.40
Latte £2.40
Flat white £2.40

MAP REF. **90**

COFFEE
4.50 / 5

OVERALL
4.50 / 5
★★★★

Dose Espresso Whitechapel

101 Back Church Lane, E1 1LU

This part of Whitechapel is a neighbourhood in flux. Once silent Victorian warehouses are being converted into covetable office space. The second Dose café occupies an expansive ground floor unit with plentiful seating. A ping pong table provides an alternative to a quiet coffee break, but it feels like the business will benefit from more time to fully realise the potential of the huge space. The Square Mile coffee is served to impeccable Dose standards and the lunch menu stars grilled cheese on sourdough served with exotic condiments such as reggae reggae sauce or bacon jam.

www.dose-espresso.com
⊖ Aldgate East

Sister locations Barbican

MON–FRI. 8:00am – 5:00pm
SAT–SUN. Closed

First opened 2014
Roaster Square Mile Coffee Roasters
Machine La Marzocco FB/80, 3 groups
Grinder Anfim, Mahlkönig EK 43

Espresso £2.00 / £2.40
Cappuccino £2.80
Latte £3.20
Flat white £2.40

MAP REF. **91**

| COFFEE 4.50 / 5 |  | OVERALL 4.25 / 5 | ★★★★✰ |

Exmouth Coffee Company

83 Whitechapel High Street, E1 7QX

In a city now peppered with cool antipodean cafés, Exmouth offers a refreshingly eclectic mixture of East End and North African influences. Situated next to Whitechapel Gallery, this lively venue attracts a diverse, arty crowd. Roasted in-house, the coffee is dark and chocolaty. Food is freshly prepared in front of customers, and extraordinarily presented. The flatbread sandwiches, quiches, and sinfully sticky pecan brownies will keep you coming back for more.

+44(0)20 7377 1010
www.exmouthcoffee.co.uk
⊖ Aldgate East / Aldgate

Sister locations Pitfield

MON–SUN. 7:30am – 8:00pm

First opened 2012
Roaster Exmouth Coffee Company
Machine La Marzocco Strada, 3 groups
Grinder Mazzer Robur, Mazzer Super Jolly

Espresso £2.00
Cappuccino £2.80
Latte £2.80
Flat white £2.80

MAP REF. **92**

| COFFEE 4.00 / 5 |  | OVERALL 4.25 / 5 | ★★★★✰ |

Fix 126

126 Curtain Road, Shoreditch, EC2A 3PJ

The second Fix location in the heart of Shoreditch is a hub of creativity and a popular place for local freelancers to meet and collaborate, or simply work alone on laptops or sketchbooks. This is also an excellent spot to stop for a daily caffeine fix, and friendly staff are happy to chat while whipping up a cup of custom-blended Climpson's espresso. A stool at one of the large front windows is the ideal place to sit and watch the comings and goings along vibrant Curtain Road.

+44(0)20 7033 9555
www.fix-coffee.co.uk
⊖ Old Street / Shoreditch High Street

Sister locations Fix

MON-FRI. 7:00am - 7:00pm
SAT-SUN. 8:00am - 7:00pm

First opened 2011
Roaster Climpson & Sons bespoke blend
Machine La Marzocco GB/5, 3 groups
Grinder Mazzer Robur E, Mazzer Super Jolly E x2

Espresso £1.60 / £2.00
Cappuccino £2.50 / £2.70
Latte £2.50 / £2.70
Flat white £2.50

MAP REF. **93**

COFFEE	OVERALL
4.25 / 5 	4.00 / 5 ★★★★☆

Full Stop

202 Brick Lane, E1 6SA

Fittingly for its location, a vintage aesthetic predominates at Full Stop, with bench seats, Formica tables and comfy sofas furnishing a long, cosy space. However, the offering here is far from antique, with fresh gourmet sandwiches and cakes providing the perfect complement to the Square Mile coffee. Visit in the evening for an interesting selection of craft beers and ciders, or tackle a weekend hangover with brunch and a Bloody Mary.

+44(0)20 7739 7086
⊖ Shoreditch High Street

MON-TUE. 7:30am - 7:00pm
WED-FRI. 7:30am - 11:00pm
SAT. 9:00am - 11:00pm
SUN. 9:00am - 9:00pm

First opened 2011
Roaster Square Mile Coffee Roasters
Machine La Marzocco GB/5, 2 groups
Grinder Anfim x2

Espresso £2.00
Cappuccino £2.80
Latte £2.80
Flat white £2.80

MAP REF. **94**

COFFEE	OVERALL
4.00 / 5 	4.00 / 5 ★★★★☆

Lantana Shoreditch

1 Oliver's Yard, 55 City Road, EC1Y 1HQ

This branch of Lantana (previously named Salvation Jane) has helped transform East London's once arid coffee landscape into a blossoming caffeine community. A takeout bar serves those in a rush, and the large midcentury-inspired casual dining room is a fashionable spot for evening meals with cocktails. Lantana's formidable brunch menu and potent Alchemy coffee (a unique blend available at Lantana only) are more than a match for even the most grievous Shoreditch hangover.

+44(0)20 7253 5273
www.lantanacafe.co.uk
⊖ Old Street

Sister locations Fitzrovia / Camden

MON. 7:30am – 4:00pm
TUE-FRI. 7:30am – 10:00pm
SAT-SUN. 9:00am – 4:00pm

First opened 2012
Roaster Alchemy bespoke blend
Machine La Marzocco FB/80, 3 groups,
La Marzocco Linea, 3 groups
Grinder Mazzer Robur E x2

Espresso £1.80 / £2.00
Cappuccino £2.60
Latte £2.60
Flat white £2.60

MAP REF. **95**

COFFEE 4.50 / 5	OVERALL 4.50 / 5
🫘🫘🫘🫘🫘	★★★★⯪

Lyle's

Tea Building, 56 Shoreditch High Street, E1 6JJ

With a few exceptions, restaurants are guilty of some grievous crimes against coffee. At Lyle's you can eat very handsomely (seasonal, unfussy fare) and conclude your meal with a jaw-dropping espresso. If you're in the mood for a coffee and nothing more, that's fine too: the bar, overseen by talented barista, James Low, is an all-day affair offering exceptional beans from the likes of Sweden's Koppi and Belleville from Paris. At Lyle's, coffee is treated with the same respect as food and wine, challenging entrenched perceptions of how restaurants think about coffee.

+44(0)20 3011 5911
www.lyleslondon.com
⊖ Shoreditch High Street

MON–FRI. 8:00am – 11:00pm
SAT. 6:00pm – 11:00pm
SUN. Closed

First opened 2014
Roaster Belleville, Koppi and guests
Machine Nuova Simonelli Aurelia II T3, 2 groups
Grinder Mahlkönig EK 43

Espresso £2.30
Cappuccino £2.60
Latte £2.70
Flat white £2.60

MAP REF. **96**

 COFFEE 4.50 / 5 **OVERALL** 4.50 / 5

Nude Espresso Hanbury Street

26 Hanbury Street, E1 6QR

Photo courtesy of the venue

Located close to the bustling Spitalfields and Brick Lane markets, Nude Espresso is one of London's busiest weekend destinations for coffee lovers. Nude offers much more than just a pit stop for weekend shoppers, with its famous 'East' espresso blend and hearty brunch options making it well worth braving the mobs any day of the week. The Nude Roastery itself is just across the road, for anyone who is interested to learn more about the coffee-making process.

+44(0)7712 899 335
www.nudeespresso.com
⊖ Shoreditch High Street / Liverpool Street

Sister locations Soho / Nude Espresso Roastery

MON–FRI. 7:00am – 6:00pm
SAT–SUN. 9:30am – 5:00pm

First opened 2008
Roaster Nude Coffee Roasters
Machine La Marzocco FB/80, 3 groups
Grinder Nuova Simonelli Mythos,
Compak K-10 x3

Espresso £2.20
Cappuccino £2.80
Latte £2.80
Flat white £2.80

MAP REF. **97**

COFFEE 4.75 / 5	OVERALL 4.50 / 5 ★★★★✬

Nude Espresso Roastery

25 Hanbury Street, E1 6QR

The Nude Espresso Roastery relocated to these premises after outgrowing its original site. Situated opposite the Nude café, the Roastery's giant floor to ceiling windows provide a prime view of the hip crowds circling the Old Truman Brewery. Nude beans are roasted in small batches on their 35kg Loring Smart roaster, keeping the coffee company's three venues and growing list of independent coffee bars well supplied. Visit the roastery to learn about the process of coffee selection, roasting and tasting from those who know it best.

+44(0)7804 223 590
www.nudeespresso.com
Shoreditch High Street / Liverpool Street

Sister locations Soho / Hanbury Street

MON-TUE. Closed
WED-FRI. 9:00am - 5:00pm
SAT-SUN. 11:00am - 6:00pm

First opened 2008
Roaster Nude Coffee Roasters
Machine La Marzocco FB/80, 3 groups
Grinder Nuova Simonelli Mythos,
Compak K-10 x3

Espresso £2.20
Cappuccino £2.80
Latte £2.80
Flat white £2.80

MAP REF. **98**

 COFFEE 4.75 / 5  OVERALL 4.50 / 5 ★★★★✦

Ozone Coffee Roasters

11 Leonard Street, EC2A 4AQ

Photo: Gary Handley

Three years in the making, this huge dual-level roastery, café and bar is a stunning addition to London's coffee scene. A central island on the first floor contains an open kitchen, around which are arrayed bar stools where customers can sip a brew and watch their food being prepared. Further seating is provided downstairs, in view of the magnificent Probat roaster. Ozone's decor is a combination of Victorian industrial, Kiwi kitsch and South American barrio, resulting in a contemporary yet welcoming atmosphere that exudes an overarching passion for coffee.

+44(0)20 7490 1039
www.ozonecoffee.co.uk
Old Street

MON-FRI. 7:30am - 6:00pm
SAT-SUN. 9:00am - 5:00pm

First opened 2012
Roaster Ozone Coffee Roasters
Machine La Marzocco Strada, 3 groups
Grinder Mahlkönig EK 43, Mazzer Robur, Mazzer Kold

Espresso £2.00
Cappuccino £2.80
Latte £2.80
Flat white £2.80

MAP REF. 99

COFFEE 4.75 / 5	OVERALL 5 / 5

113

Shoreditch Grind

213 Old Street, EC1V 9NR

Photo: Gary Handley

With its retro cinema signage, circular interior and prime location right on the Old Street 'Silicon' roundabout, Shoreditch Grind is coffee theatre at its finest. Coffee lovers can sit on bar stools and look out at one of the city's busiest transport hubs while feeling insulated from the rat race with a cup of delicious custom-blended coffee in hand. As the Shoreditch night draws in, the café transforms into a hip bar serving beers, wines and cocktails. The venue also has a recording studio which is available for musicians to hire.

+44(0)20 7490 7490
www.shoreditchgrind.com
⊖ Old Street (Exit 8)

Sister locations Soho Grind / Holborn Grind

MON-THU. 7:00am - 11:00pm
FRI. 7:00am - 1:00am
SAT. 8:00am - 1:00am
SUN. 9:00am - 6:00pm

First opened 2011
Roaster Small Batch Coffee Company bespoke blend
Machine La Marzocco Linea PB, 2 groups x2
Grinder La Marzocco Vulcano x2

Espresso £2.20
Cappuccino £2.70 / £3.00
Latte £2.70 / £3.00
Flat white £2.70 / £3.00

MAP REF. **100**

COFFEE 4.50 / 5		OVERALL 4.50 / 5	

Slate Coffee

96 Curtain Road, EC2A 3AA

Slate chalks up another win for speciality coffee in hipster-happy Shoreditch. The small, but punchy space is splashed with vivid graphics, completely in keeping with Curtain Road's edgy street art. Food arrives plated on slates, which perfectly match the custom painted stone grey La Marzocco espresso machine. If you prefer a mellow coffee, a rotating filter brew is also on offer. Slate has worked wonders with the space, and is proving a welcome addition to the area's creative coffee community.

+44 (0)20 3620 6980
www.slatecoffeelondon.co.uk
⊖ Shoreditch High Street / Old Street

MON–FRI. 8:00am – 7:00pm
SAT–SUN. 10:00am – 6:00pm

First opened 2013
Roaster Allpress Espresso
Machine La Marzocco FB/80, 2 groups
Grinder Mazzer Royal

Espresso £1.80 / £2.10
Cappuccino £2.80
Latte £2.80
Flat white £2.50

MAP REF. **101**

Trade

47 Commercial Street, E1 6BD

Trade is a neatly pulled together outfit among the textile wholesalers of Spitalfields, dealing in stout sandwiches and a no-nonsense approach to coffee making. The painted brick walls and industrial fittings may be rather hackneyed, but the interior is well-planned, spacious and wholly redeemed by a sun splashed terrace. Prepare to reckon with bold brunch and lunch options including formidable lobster rolls and reuben sandwiches. Boasting walloping fare and well-made coffee, Trade is a juicy morsel on an otherwise unappetising strip of Commercial Street.

+44(0)20 3490 1880
www.trade-made.co.uk
⊖ Aldgate East

MON-FRI. 7:30am - 5:00pm
SAT-SUN. 10:00am - 5:00pm

First opened 2014
Roaster Origin Coffee and guests
Machine Orchestrale Etnica, 2 groups
Grinder Mazzer Major E, Mazzer Super Jolly E

Espresso £1.80
Cappuccino £2.40
Latte £2.40
Flat white £2.40

MAP REF.

 **COFFEE** 4.25 / 5

 **OVERALL** 4.50 / 5 ★★★★✬

White Mulberries

D3 Ivory House, St Katharine Docks, E1W 1AT

Like its namesake, White Mulberries is a sweet find; a rare combination of beautiful setting and great coffee. Located in St Katharine Docks - London's little-known marina - visitors have an enviable view of the swan-like sailboats. The café really comes into its own in fine weather when outdoor seating is provided overlooking the water. Customers are treated to a rotating range of beans from top UK and international microroasters. Accompany your coffee with an award winning 'super moist' brownie.

www.whitemulberries.com
Tower Hill / Tower Gateway DLR

MON-FRI. 7:30am - 5:00pm
SAT-SUN. 8:00am - 5:00pm

First opened 2012
Roaster Rotating roasters
Machine La Marzocco FB/80, 2 groups
Grinder Mazzer Major, Mazzer Super Jolly

Espresso £2.00
Cappuccino £2.80 / £3.10
Latte £2.70 / £3.00
Flat white £2.80 / £3.10

MAP REF. 103

COFFEE 4.50 / 5	OVERALL 4.25 / 5

117

East

East London has successfully shaken off its label as a rough outer region to emerge as London's booming artistic neighbourhood. A wonderful combination of cultures and a thriving creative scene have helped put the area back on the map, and provide a fertile environment for London's coffee pioneers.

119 Lower Clapton

119 Lower Clapton Road, E5 0NP

Lower Clapton Road once attracted the unfortunate moniker 'Murder Mile' for its high rate of crime. Now the formerly unloved E5 postcode has received a visit from the gentrification fairy (along with an influx of creatives seeking reasonable rents). Thanks to the floor to ceiling windows and whitewashed walls, 119 feels infinitely light and airy. Local owner Erica Routledge has transformed the space into a quality neighbourhood café that longstanding and newly-arrived Clapton residents can all be rightly proud of.

+44(0)20 8533 9763
www.119lowerclapton.co.uk
⊖ Hackney Central

MON-FRI. 8:00am - 5:30pm
SAT. 9:00am - 5:00pm
SUN. 10:00am - 4:00pm

First opened 2013
Roaster Workshop Coffee Co.
Machine Nuova Simonelli Aurelia II, 2 groups
Grinder Mazzer Major, Mahlkönig Vario

Espresso £2.00
Cappuccino £2.60
Latte £2.60
Flat white £2.60

MAP REF. 104

COFFEE 4.25 / 5

OVERALL 4.00 / 5 ★ ★ ★ ★ ☆

46b Espresso Hut

46b Brooksby's Walk, E9 6DA

Photo courtesy of the venue

Locals should seriously consider altering their morning commute expressly to visit 46b. Visitors from elsewhere will discover some of the best coffee served in Hackney in this unassuming, yet enchanting café. The zesty Red Brick blend pulled through the Seattle-made Synesso Cyncra is worth travelling for. Scrupulously selected suppliers include Northiam Dairy, E5 Bakehouse, and London Borough of Jam. 46b is Hackney's quietly brilliant venue.

+44(0)7702 063 172
www.46b-espressohut.co.uk
⊖ Homerton

MON–FRI. 7:30am – 6:30pm
SAT. 9:00am – 6:30pm
SUN. 10:00am – 6:00pm

First opened 2012
Roaster Square Mile Coffee Roasters
Machine Synesso Cyncra, 2 groups
Grinder Anfim Super Caimano, Mazzer Super Jolly

Espresso £2.00
Cappuccino £2.40
Latte £2.40
Flat white £2.40

MAP REF.

COFFEE 4.50 / 5	OVERALL 4.25 / 5
🫘🫘🫘🫘🫘	★★★★✫

56 St James

56 St James Street, E17 7PE

56 St James is a true neighbourhood coffee shop. There's something for everyone here: delicious coffee, the large communal table, a gigantic chalkboard for children and cakes handmade by none other than the owner's mum. This café also has a penchant for pineapples: pineapple themed art cheerfully graces the walls and visitors are greeted by an enormous pineapple donning the exterior brickwork. In past centuries, this exotic fruit was a symbol of prosperity. 56 St James is a sure sign that Walthamstow's fortunes are on the up.

+44(0)7792 328 479
≥ St James Street

MON-TUE. Closed
WED-FRI. 9:00am - 6:00pm
SAT-SUN. 10:00am - 6:00pm

First opened 2014
Roaster Nude Espresso
Machine La Marzocco Linea, 2 groups
Grinder Compak K-10, Compak K-3

Espresso £2.00
Cappuccino £2.50
Latte £2.50
Flat white £2.50

MAP REF.

Climpson & Sons

67 Broadway Market, E8 4PH

Photo: Gary Handley

East

Revered by coffee lovers in East London and beyond, the Climpson & Sons café has developed into one of the biggest names in London coffee. You'll be lucky to even make it through the door of the café while Broadway Market is in full swing on Saturdays. The company's impressive new Loring roaster is housed nearby at Climpson's Arch on Helmsley Place. From Thursdays to Sundays, the roastery transforms into an informal drinking and dining venue, hosting supper clubs and summer barbecues.

+44(0)20 7812 9829
www.climpsonandsons.com
⊖ Haggerston / ⇄ Cambridge Heath Rail

Sister locations Broadway Market Stall
(Sat only) / Climpson Arch (Thu-Sun)

MON-FRI. 7:30am - 5:00pm
SAT. 8:30am - 5:00pm
SUN. 9:00am - 5:00pm

First opened 2005
Roaster Climpson & Sons
Machine La Marzocco PB, 3 groups
Grinder Mahlkönig EK 43, Anfim

Espresso £2.00
Cappuccino £2.60 / £2.80
Latte £2.60 / £2.80
Flat white £2.60

MAP REF. 107

Cooper & Wolf

145 Chatsworth Road, E5 0LA

Occupying a sunny spot on gentrifying Chatsworth Road, Cooper & Wolf's Swedish charm is irresistible. Curious Scandinavian ornaments peep out from between potted plants, and lilting Nordic accents punctuate the atmosphere. Caravan coffee is exquisitely served by Alex and barista James, while co-owner Sara heads up a kitchen offering delicious Swedish dishes, many from old family recipes. The råraka with Hansen & Lydersen salmon makes a particularly delicious accompaniment to a morning cappuccino.

www.cooperandwolf.co.uk
⊖ Homerton / ⇌ Clapton Rail

MON-THU. 9:00am - 5:30pm
FRI. 9:00am - 6:00pm
SAT-SUN. 10:00am - 6:00pm

First opened 2012
Roaster Caravan
Machine Synesso Cyncra, 2 groups
Grinder Mazzer Super Jolly, Anfim Super Caimano, Mahlkönig Tanzania

Espresso £2.00
Cappuccino £2.40
Latte £2.40
Flat white £2.40

MAP REF.

COFFEE
4.25 / 5

OVERALL
4.25 / 5
★ ★ ★ ★ ⯪

Counter Café and Roastery

Stour Space, 7 Roach Road, E3 2PA

Photo courtesy of the venue

Counter Café and Roastery is situated within Hackney Wick's Stour Space gallery, with a gorgeous view directly onto the canal. The smashed brick walls and signature vintage cinema seats lend the interior a grungy charm. The café roasts its own beans on a beautiful San Franciscan roaster, proudly displayed at the rear of the space. Nearby sister business, Crate Brewery, keeps local artists well supplied with craft beer and pizza. Counter Café and Roastery is a unique venue bursting with creative spirit; well worth the journey east.

+44(0)7834 275 920
www.counterproductive.co.uk
⊖ Hackney Wick

Sister locations Crate Brewery

MON-FRI. 7:45am – 5:00pm
SAT-SUN. 9:00am – 5:00pm

First opened 2009
Roaster Counter Roastery
Machine Synesso Cyncra, 2 groups
Grinder Anfim

Espresso £1.80
Cappuccino £2.50
Latte £2.50
Flat white £2.50

MAP REF. **109**

COFFEE 4.50 / 5	OVERALL 4.50 / 5	★★★★½

Craving Coffee

Gaunson House, 3 Markfield Road, N15 4QQ

Craving Coffee began life as a coffee cart and now finds a permanent home in a converted industrial unit shared with The Mill Co. studios. Co-owner, Matt Ho, formerly worked for roasters Climpson & Sons and Union, and his experience clearly shines through in the superb coffee service. The kitchen turns out thoughtfully-prepared dishes using ingredients from local suppliers, such as smoked salmon from House of Sverre. This large, versatile space presents plenty of opportunity for events including art exhibitions, supper clubs and coffee brewing masterclasses.

+44(0)20 8808 3178
www.cravingcoffee.co.uk
⊖ Seven Sisters / Tottenham Hale

MON-SUN. 10:00am - 5:00pm

First opened 2014
Roaster Weanie Beans
Machine La Marzocco GB/5, 2 groups
Grinder Anfim Super Caimano x2, Macap

Espresso £2.00
Cappuccino £2.50
Latte £2.50
Flat white £2.50

MAP REF.

COFFEE 4.50 / 5 **OVERALL** 4.25 / 5

Dreyfus

19 Lower Clapton Road, E5 0NS

Photo courtesy of the venue

Every walk of East London life is represented at this Hackney hangout. The clean Northern European-style decor mixed with a dash of Americana, such as the comfortable booth seating, creates an easy-going environment. A mix of students, families, freelancers and the occasional canine come here for the reasonably priced - yet well made - coffee and hearty food. Egg stacks can be mixed and matched from a range of classics like Benedict, Royale or the more unconventional Leopold (the house special).

+44(0)20 8985 4311
www.dreyfuscafe.co.uk
⊖ Hackney Central / ⇌ Hackney Downs Rail

MON-FRI. 8:00am - 6:00pm
SAT-SUN. 9:00am - 5:00pm

First opened 2012
Roaster Has Bean
Machine San Remo Verona, 2 groups
Grinder Mahlkönig K 30 Vario

Espresso £2.00
Cappuccino £2.50 / £2.80
Latte £2.50 / £2.80
Flat white £2.40

MAP REF. **111**

Embassy East

285 Hoxton Street, N1 5JX

Behind the plain exterior and nondescript street address, Embassy East is a café with real soul. Opened on a modest budget, the visitor soon senses the love and ingenuity invested by the founding friends, Chris Coleman and Tommy Studholme (formerly of Flat White). It's the small things that make this Hoxton coffee bar special, like the cleverly modified coffee grinder and quirky pickle jar light fittings. The open kitchen offers carefully prepared breakfast and lunch made fresh with artisanal ingredients.

+44(0)20 7739 8340
www.embassyeast.co.uk
⊖ Hoxton

MON–FRI. 9:00am – 6:00pm
SAT–SUN. 10:00am – 6:00pm

First opened 2013
Roaster Workshop Coffee Co.
Machine La Marzocco Linea, 3 groups
Grinder Anfim, Mahlkönig Columbia

Espresso £2.00
Cappuccino £2.50
Latte £2.70
Flat white £2.50

MAP REF. 112

COFFEE 4.50 / 5  OVERALL 4.25 / 5

Esters

55 Kynaston Road, N16 0EB

Stoke Newington residents are fortunate to have such a brilliant little neighbourhood coffee shop on their doorstep. Standing on the site formerly occupied by café Fred & Fran, owners Nia and Jack have created a sanctum where everyone is welcome, from coffee geeks to mums. The food is outstanding and the aforementioned coffee geeks will be delighted to sample two different filter coffees in addition to espresso-based drinks.

+44(0)20 7254 0253
www.estersn16.com
⇌ Rectory Road Rail /
Stoke Newington Rail

MON. Closed
TUE-FRI. 8:00am - 5:00pm
SAT. 9:00am - 5:00pm
SUN. 10:00am - 4:00pm

First opened 2013
Roaster Has Bean and guests
Machine La Marzocco Linea, 2 groups
Grinder Nuova Simonelli Mythos One, Mahlkönig EK 43

Espresso £2.20
Cappuccino £2.60
Latte £2.80
Flat white £2.60

MAP REF. **113**

 COFFEE 4.50 / 5

 OVERALL 4.25 / 5 ★★★★⯪

Fabrique Bakery

Arch 385, Geffrye Street, E2 8HZ

Bakery café Fabrique is a cinnamon-sprinkled slice of Stockholm nestled in a railway arch near Hoxton station. The Swedish coffee break, known as fika, is a national institution almost always involving baked goods, and the sweeter the better. So it's just as well that Fabrique's artisan bakers are revered for their decadent buns, bejewelled with sugar crystals and doused with cinnamon or cardamom. The coffee is crafted with beans from Johan & Nyström, a highly respected Nordic artisan roaster.

+44(0)20 7033 0268
www.fabrique.co.uk
⊖ Hoxton

MON-FRI. 8:00am - 6:00pm
SAT-SUN. 10:00am - 6:00pm

First opened 2012
Roaster Johan & Nyström
Machine Dalla Corte, 3 groups
Grinder Mahlkönig K 30

Espresso £1.75 / £2.00
Cappuccino £2.50 / £2.75
Latte £2.75
Flat white £2.50

MAP REF.

COFFEE
3.75 / 5

OVERALL
4.00 / 5

Foxcroft & Ginger Whitechapel

69-79 Mile End Road, E1 4TT

Whitechapel's tech startup scene is surging. Creative companies are pouring in, and so are the trendy flat whites. Foxcroft & Ginger's dramatic new East End destination fronts an outpost of Central Working, a space for entrepreneurs to grow their businesses. But this café provides much more than just caffeine for coders. Expect a mighty brunch and lunch service with steaming plates of pulled pork and famous F&G sourdough pizza. Stick around and join the late night hackers for a glass of Camden Pale Ale while you hustle for your next killer app idea.

www.foxcroftandginger.co.uk
⊖ Whitechapel / Stepney Green

Sister locations Soho

MON–FRI. 8:00am - 10:00pm
SAT. 9:00am - 10:00pm
SUN. 9:00am - 7:00pm

First opened 2014
Roaster The Roasting Party
Machine La Marzocco Linea, 2 groups
Grinder Mazzer Robur, Anfim

Espresso £2.20
Cappuccino £2.50
Latte £2.50 / £2.80
Flat white £2.50

MAP REF.

COFFEE 4.50 / 5   🫘🫘🫘🫘🫘   **OVERALL** 4.50 / 5   ★★★★⯪

131

G&T

204 Cambridge Heath Road, E2 9NQ

This tiny coffee house and deli is the passion project of Italian couple Marco and Ilaria, who serve lovingly prepared Square Mile coffee to the artists and passersby on busy Cambridge Heath Road. G&T also offer cold-pressed juices and a carefully selected range of organic, locally sourced produce and vegan foods. Cakes and pastries sit alongside bottles of Italian pasta sauce, preserves and artisanal bread baked just up the road at E5 Bakehouse.

+44(0)7956 355 145
www.gandtlondon.co.uk
≋ Cambridge Heath Rail /
⊖ Bethnal Green

MON-FRI. 8:00am - 4:00pm
SAT-SUN. 9:00am - 4:00pm

First opened 2011
Roaster Square Mile Coffee Roasters
Machine Rancilio Classe 9 Xcelsius, 2 groups
Grinder Anfim Super Caimano,

Espresso £2.00
Cappuccino £2.50
Latte £2.50
Flat white £2.50

MAP REF. ⑪⑥

COFFEE 4.25 / 5		OVERALL 4.00 / 5	

Grind Coffee Bar Westfield Stratford City

Lower ground floor, Westfield Stratford, E20 1EJ

A vast shopping mall is the last place you'd expect to find great coffee, but tucked away down one end of Westfield Stratford is an outpost of Putney café Grind. The venue occupies a large, open-plan space designed to provide a respite from the bedlam of the shopping mall with kitchen-style tables, leather wingback chairs and a soothing New Zealand theme. Coffee is tailored for busy shoppers but more serious options are also available in the form of guest espressos and single-origin filters.

www.grindcoffeebar.co.uk
⊖ Stratford

Sister locations Putney

MON-FRI. 8:00am - 9:00pm
SAT. 9:00am - 9:00pm
SUN. 11:00am - 6:00pm

First opened 2011
Roaster Grind Roast Works
Machine La Marzocco Strada EP, 3 groups
Grinder Mazzer Robur x2

Espresso £1.80
Cappuccino £2.30 / £2.70 / £2.90
Latte £2.30 / £2.70 / £2.90
Flat white £2.30 / £2.70 / 2.90

MAP REF. ⑪⑦

COFFEE 4.25 / 5		OVERALL 4.00 / 5	

The Hackney Pearl

11 Prince Edward Road, E9 5LX

Hidden away in the Hackney Wick industrial area, The Hackney Pearl rewards the urban explorer with simple, yet delicious coffee and food. The Pearl serves as a hub for the growing community of local artists, many of whom work in studios nearby. The broad glass shopfront admits plenty of natural light, and outdoor seating is also plentiful. The beautiful seasonal menu changes daily and an extensive bar list is also available. The Pearl is open until late every evening for dinner, drinks and events.

+44(0)20 8510 3605
www.thehackneypearl.com
⊖ Hackney Wick

MON–SAT. 10:00am – 11:00pm
SUN. 10:00am – 8:00pm

First opened 2009
Roaster Ozone Coffee Roasters
Machine La Marzzoco FB/80, 3 groups
Grinder Mazzer Major, Mazzer Super Jolly

Espresso £1.80 / £2.10
Cappuccino £2.20 / £2.50
Latte £2.20 / £2.50
Flat white £2.20 / £2.50

MAP REF. **118**

 COFFEE 4.00 / 5   **OVERALL** 4.00 / 5   ★★★★☆

Haggerston Espresso Room

Unit C, 13 Downham Road, N1 5AA

Haggerston Espresso Room, or HER as this Dalston darling likes to be known, is a sweetheart of the Hackney creative brigade. The mismatched furniture is a combination of school classroom and grandmother chic, which is sure to suit East End fashionistas down to the ground (quite literally; the sofas boast considerable sag). Fortunately the Climpsons coffee is no slouch, and the 'sexy toast' contributes to a seductive food menu. HER is a characterful café with a sense of humour you can't help but like.

+44(0)20 7249 0880
⊖ Haggerston

MON–FRI. 7:30am – 6:00pm
SAT. 9:00am – 6:00pm
SUN. 10:00am – 6:00pm

First opened 2011
Roaster Climpson & Sons
Machine La Marzocco Linea, 3 groups
Grinder Mazzer Royal, Mazzer Super Jolly

Espresso £2.10
Cappuccino £2.60 / £3.00
Latte £2.60 / £3.00
Flat white £2.60

MAP REF. **119**

 COFFEE 4.00 / 5       **OVERALL** 4.00 / 5   ★★★★☆

Lanark

262 Hackney Road, E2 7SJ

Lanark is a little slip of a coffee bar named after Alasdair Gray's dystopian novel. Don't expect to find frivolities like tea or soya milk here, but you can rely on owner, Greg Boyce, to fix you a superb brew with an assortment of beans from top microroasters. Coffee geeks will gravitate towards the Victoria Arduino Athena, a mythological lever-operated espresso machine with beautiful hammered metalwork and exquisite detailing. Lanark is a coffee bar with particular appeal to London's coffee purists.

www.lanarkcoffee.co.uk
⊖ Hoxton

MON. Closed
TUE-FRI. 8:00am - 4:00pm
SAT-SUN. 10:00am - 4:00pm

First opened 2014
Roaster Alchemy and guests
Machine Victoria Arduino Athena Leva, 2 groups
Grinder Mahlkönig EK 43

Espresso £2.00
Cappuccino £2.50
Latte £2.50
Flat white £2.50

MAP REF. 120

 COFFEE 4.50 / 5

 OVERALL 4.25 / 5 ★★★★⯪

Look Mum No Hands! Hackney

125-127 Mare Street, E8 3RH

More commuters choose to cycle than drive to work in Hackney. As one of its main arteries, Mare Street at times resembles a stage from Le Tour de France. It's the perfect location then, for the second Look Mum No Hands! cycle-themed café. With more space on the bar, there's a greater range of coffees on offer than at the first Old Street venue. What's more, there's a particularly tempting line up of craft beers on tap, although cyclists may want to sober up with an espresso before returning to Mare Street's traffic madness.

+44(0)7985 200 472
www.lookmumnohands.com
⇌ London Fields Rail

Sister locations Clerkenwell

MON-TUE. 8:00am - 8:00pm
WED-FRI. 8:00am - 10:00pm
SAT. 9:00am - 10:00pm
SUN. 9:30am - 10:00pm

First opened 2013
Roaster Square Mile Coffee Roasters and guests
Machine Kees van der Westen Mirage, 3 groups
Grinder Anfim Barista x2, Mahlkönig EK 43

Espresso £2.00
Cappuccino £2.60
Latte £2.60
Flat white £2.60

MAP REF. **121**

COFFEE 4.50 / 5	🫘🫘🫘🫘🫘	OVERALL 4.50 / 5	★★★★⯪

Mission

250 Paradise Row, E2 9LE

Mission's sister bar, Sager + Wilde, upended snooty wine bar stereotypes when it opened in a former East End boozer in 2013. Snuck into a Bethnal Green railway arch, Mission exudes the same unpretentious yet grown-up atmosphere. What's more, it offers a coffee service every inch as considered as the Californian-driven wine and food menu. Drafting in the expertise of Michael Cleland (formerly of Sharps), coffee and tea are no afterthought, but an equally valuable part of the palette of flavours colouring this slice of aptly named Paradise Row.

+44(0)20 7613 0478
www.missione2.com
◯ Bethnal Green

Sister locations Sager + Wilde

MON. 6:00pm - 12:00am
TUE-FRI. 12:00pm - 12:00am
SAT-SUN. 10:00am - 12:00am

First opened 2014
Roaster Square Mile Coffee Roasters, Workshop Coffee Co. and guests
Machine Victoria Arduino Athena Leva, 3 groups
Grinder Anfim, Mahlkönig Tanzania

Espresso £2.00
Cappuccino £2.50
Latte £2.50
Flat white £2.50

MAP REF.

 COFFEE 4.50 / 5  OVERALL 4.50 / 5

Mouse & De Lotz

103 Shacklewell Lane, E8 2EB

To enter Mouse & De Lotz is to step back in time to an era of glass milk bottles, Singer sewing machines and cakes made by hand. Squashy sofas, window seats and a pretty, vintage aesthetic enhance the comforting retro feel, but free wifi brings this café right up to date and makes it an ideal place to spend a lazy hour. Superb coffee is prepared by a rotating staff of artists, students and parents, all of whom bring full-time passion to the food and drinks they prepare for their Dalston customers.

+44(0)20 3489 8082
www.mousedelotz.com
⊖ Dalston Kingsland

MON-FRI. 8:00am - 5:00pm
SAT. 9:00am - 5:00pm
SUN. 10:00am - 5:00pm

First opened 2010
Roaster Square Mile Coffee Roasters
Machine La Marzocco Linea, 2 groups
Grinder Mazzer Super Jolly E, Anfim

Espresso £2.00
Cappuccino £2.40
Latte £2.40
Flat white £2.40

MAP REF.

| COFFEE 4.00 / 5 | | OVERALL 4.00 / 5 | ★★★★☆ |

Pavilion

Victoria Park, Crown Gate West, E9 7DE

Perfectly positioned overlooking a beautiful lake, Pavilion offers excellent coffee and fresh food to the crowds of locals who flock to Victoria Park every day to walk their dogs, exercise, spend time with family or simply relax. The café itself features a striking domed glass roof and the outdoor decking area offers stunning views over the lake and park. Pavilion's popular brunch menu is organic and locally sourced wherever possible. The British-style fare is best sampled on a sunny weekend, so arrive early to avoid the queue.

+44(0)20 8980 0030
www.the-pavilion-cafe.com
⊖ Bethnal Green / Mile End

Sister locations Elliots

MON-SUN. 8:00am - 4:00pm

First opened 2007
Roaster Square Mile Coffee Roasters
Machine Synesso Cyncra, 3 groups
Grinder Mazzer Robur, Mazzer Super Jolly

Espresso £2.00
Cappuccino £2.50
Latte £2.50
Flat white £2.50

MAP REF.

| COFFEE 4.25 / 5 | | OVERALL 4.25 / 5 | ★★★★☆ |

Reilly Rocket

507 Kingsland Road, E8 4AU

Situated behind a motorcycle shop, Reilly Rocket is the antidote to twee, chintzy cafés and industrial chic. Decorated with colourful memorabilia, brown leather sofas, taxidermy and graphic wall art, Reilly's is a haven for lovers of rebellion and retro road culture. Hunter S. Thompson would have been right at home here. The coffee is just as gutsy and is pulled by a team of hardcore baristas. If you're in need of further fuel, the Antipodean-inspired brunch menu will soon have you firing on all cylinders.

www.reillyrocket.com
⊖ Dalston Junction

MON-FRI. 8:00am - 5:00pm
SAT. 9:00am - 5:00pm
SUN. 10:00am - 5:00pm

First opened 2011
Roaster Square Mile Coffee Roasters
Machine La Marzocco Linea, 2 groups
Grinder Anfim

Espresso £1.80
Cappuccino £2.60
Latte £2.50
Flat white £2.50

MAP REF.

 **COFFEE** 4.25 / 5

 **OVERALL** 4.00 / 5 ★★★★☆

Taylor St Baristas Canary Wharf

8 South Colonnade, Canary Wharf, E14 4PZ

Photo courtesy of the venue

East

This lean, mean café is designed to produce a high volume of quality coffee for the district's bankers and business people. The venue is predominantly set up to serve takeaway drinks, but there are also a small number of tables. In addition to espresso-based drinks, customers can opt for a single origin coffee brewed by AeroPress. A full breakfast menu is on offer complemented by cakes and Australian classics such as lamingtons, and cheese and Vegemite muffins.

+44(0)20 7519 6536
www.taylor-st.com
⊖ Canary Wharf

Sister locations Liverpool Street / Shoreditch / Monument / Bank / Mayfair / South Quay

MON-FRI. 7:00am - 6:00pm
SAT-SUN. Closed

First opened 2011
Roaster Union Hand-Roasted and guests
Machine Nuova Simonelli Aurelia II, 3 groups x2, Synesso Cyncra, 2 groups
Grinder Mazzer Robur E x2, Mazzer Major E x2, Anfim, Mahlkönig Tanzania

Espresso £1.80
Cappuccino £2.50 / £2.90
Latte £2.50 / £2.90
Flat white £2.50 / £3.40

MAP REF. 126

| COFFEE 4.50 / 5 | 🫘 🫘 🫘 🫘 🫘 | OVERALL 4.25 / 5 | ★ ★ ★ ★ ⯪ |

139

Taylor St Baristas South Quay

1 Harbour Exchange Square, E14 9GE

London's financial district runs on regular doses of caffeine, administered by the skilled hands of Taylor St's dedicated baristas. This large café offers both a rapid takeaway service and ample seating; ideal for conducting casual business meetings. The timber-clad counter is stacked with healthy salads and antipodean treats such as ANZAC biscuits. At South Quay, Taylor St pulls off exceptional coffee and food within the constraints of a very busy site. With £1.8 million crowd-funded investment, this ambitious coffee company is embarking on an exciting new phase of expansion.

+44(0)20 3069 8833
www.taylor-st.com
● South Quay

Sister locations Liverpool Street / Shoreditch / Canary Wharf / Monument / Mayfair / Bank

MON–FRI. 8:00am – 5:00pm
SAT–SUN. Closed

First opened 2013
Roaster Union Hand-Roasted and guests
Machine Nuova Simonelli Aurelia II T3, 3 groups
Grinder Nuova Simonelli Mythos, Mazzer Robur, Anfim, Mahlkönig Tanzania

Espresso £1.80 / £2.30
Cappuccino £2.50 / £2.90
Latte £2.50 / £2.90
Flat white £2.50 / £3.40

MAP REF.

COFFEE 4.50 / 5

OVERALL 4.25 / 5

Tina, We Salute You

47 King Henry's Walk, N1 4NH

Dalston locals are fiercely protective of Tina, We Salute You. The enigmatic Tina presides over a lush selection of tarts, cakes, sticky buns and glorious coffee. The corner location provides the perfect location to soak up the afternoon sun while engrossed in a magazine. The interior is regularly given over to creatives to use as an exhibition space, and one of the outside walls hosts street art by local artists. An eagerly anticipated second Tina location is due to open in 2015 in Stratford.

+44(0)20 3119 0047
www.tinawesaluteyou.com
⊖ Dalston Kingsland

MON–FRI. 8:00am – 6:00pm
SAT–SUN. 10:00am – 7:00pm

First opened 2009
Roaster The Roasting Shed, Alchemy
Machine La Marzocco Linea, 3 groups
Grinder Anfim

Espresso £2.00
Cappuccino £2.80
Latte £2.80
Flat white £2.80

MAP REF. **128**

COFFEE 4.50 / 5		OVERALL 4.25 / 5	★ ★ ★ ★ ⯪

Wilton Way Café

63 Wilton Way, E8 1BG

Wilton Way Café combines superb coffee and fresh, simple food with art and music to create a memorable experience. With its clever modular furniture, rotating art exhibits, busy coffee bar, generous display of cakes and a radio corner producing live local broadcasts, Wilton's makes excellent use of its intimate but vibrant space. Visit on a sunny Saturday to enjoy a fine cup of coffee on the footpath outside, along with the Wilton Way faithful.

www.londonfieldsradio.co.uk/the-cafe
⊖ Hackney Central /
⇌ Hackney Downs Rail

MON–FRI. 8:00am – 5:00pm
SAT–SUN. 9:00am – 6:00pm

First opened 2009
Roaster Climpson & Sons
Machine La Marzocco Linea, 2 groups
Grinder Mazzer Super Jolly, Anfim

Espresso £2.00
Cappuccino £2.50 / £2.70
Latte £2.50 / £2.70
Flat white £2.50

MAP REF. **129**

COFFEE 4.25 / 5		OVERALL 4.50 / 5	★ ★ ★ ★ ⯪

Wood St Coffee

Blackhorse Workshop, 1-2 Sutherland Road Path, E17 6BX

Walthamstow has its grimier moments, but mostly it's known for its strong community, green spaces and, like other gentrifying areas, a growing thirst for coffee. Wood St Coffee has an authentic feel, housed in the proudly blue collar Blackhorse Workshops, busy with metalworkers, carpenters, bakers and brewers. Come here for honest, well made coffee enjoyed with slabs of sourdough toast baked fresh on site. The building isn't easy to locate (hidden down an alley off Blackhorse Lane), but the explorer's persistence will be amply rewarded.

+44(0)7944 888 011
www.woodstcoffee.co.uk
⊖ Blackhorse Road

MON-SAT. 9:00am – 5:00pm
SUN. Closed

First opened 2014
Roaster Climpson & Sons, Weenie Beans, Counter Roastery
Machine Wega Atlas, 2 groups
Grinder Mazzer Super Jolly, Mazzer Mini

Espresso £1.80
Cappuccino £2.40
Latte £2.40
Flat white £2.20

MAP REF. 130

COFFEE 4.25 / 5 | OVERALL 4.00 / 5 ★★★★☆

142

Yellow Warbler

9 Northwold Road, N16 7HL

This chirpy little café offers something genuinely different in N16. Venezuelan owner Andrea brings South American specialties to complement the Climpson & Sons coffee. Try one of the scrumptious arepas, a type of flatbread made with cornflour and filled with things like guacamole, chorizo, manchego cheese and other ingredients guaranteed to make you smile. The space is small but lively, filled with the pleasant chatter of attentive staff and their Stoke Newington regulars who flock here for the luscious food and excellent coffee.

www.yellowwarbler.co.uk
≥ Stoke Newington Rail

MON-FRI. 8:00am – 5:00pm
SAT. 9:00am – 4:30pm
SUN. 10:00am – 4:30pm

First opened 2014
Roaster Climpson & Sons
Machine La Marzocco Linea, 2 groups
Grinder Anfim, Mazzer Super Jolly

Espresso £2.00
Cappuccino £2.50
Latte £2.50
Flat white £2.50

MAP REF. 131

COFFEE 4.25 / 5	OVERALL 4.25 / 5

143

Zealand Road Coffee

391 Roman Road, E3 5QS

Roman Road seems an unlikely place to hunt for a good coffee. Located just a short walk away from leafy Victoria Park, Zealand Road Coffee's corner location is a natural sun trap and the creative locals take advantage of the laid-back atmosphere to catch up on work or a good novel. Beans are supplied by Cornwall-based Origin Coffee, which has justly earned a reputation as one of the UK's premier small batch roasters. Origin's coffee is relatively uncommon in London and worth seeking out.

+44(0)7940 235 493

Mile End / Bethnal Green

MON-SAT. 8:00am - 5:00pm
SUN. 9:00am - 5:00pm

First opened 2011
Roaster Origin Coffee
Machine La Marzocco Linea, 2 groups
Grinder Mazzer Major, Compak K-6

Espresso £1.50
Cappuccino £2.20 / £2.40
Latte £2.20 / £2.40
Flat white £2.20

MAP REF. 132

 COFFEE 4.25 / 5 OVERALL 4.00 / 5

South East

One of the capital's best kept secrets, South East London is home to a small number of quietly brilliant coffee venues, and is rapidly establishing itself on the coffee map. With the completion of the Overground line from East London to Clapham Junction via Peckham, the area is now more accessible, and rewards the urban explorer with a vibrant foodie and market scene.

Anderson & Co

139 Bellenden Road, SE15 4DH

Anderson & Co was one of the first places to offer speciality coffee in a neighbourhood now in the throes of a foodie revolution. The café-restaurant complements its coffee with artisan breads, cakes, pastries and small range of craft beer. The white, bright interior serves as a perfect canvas for the medley of tastes on offer. Tantalising aromas waft from the open kitchen to the secluded outdoor seating area at the rear. Thursday to Saturday evenings are Peckhamburger nights; expect a mouth-watering burger list beefed up with posh frites followed by ice cream sundaes.

+44(0)20 7469 7078
www.andersonandcompany.wordpress.com
Peckham Rye

MON-SAT. 8:00am - 5:00pm
SUN. 8:30am - 4:30pm

First opened 2011
Roaster Square Mile Coffee Roasters
Machine La Marzocco Linea, 2 groups
Grinder Mazzer Super Jolly, Anfim

Espresso £1.85
Cappuccino £2.50
Latte £2.50
Flat white £2.50

MAP REF. 133

 **COFFEE** 4.25 / 5  **OVERALL** 4.25 / 5 ★★★★

Arlo & Moe

340 Brockley Road, SE4 2BT

Arlo & Moe is a simply beautiful little neighbourhood café tucked away to the south of Brockley. Since opening it has struck a chord with the locals; staff and customers mingle freely as cheerful rockabilly tunes fill the air, and children are particularly welcomed. The coffee is locally roasted by Dark Fluid, and accompanied by tempting home-made food. Try the signature 'sexy toast' on campaillou bread, or meet some new friends at one of Arlo & Moe's supper nights.

+44(0)7749 667 207
Crofton Park Rail

MON-FRI. 8:00am - 4:30pm
SAT. 9:00am - 4:00pm
SUN. 10:00am - 4:00pm

First opened 2012
Roaster Dark Fluid
Machine Gaggia, 2 groups
Grinder Mazzer Super Jolly

Espresso £2.00
Cappuccino £2.50 / £3.10
Latte £2.50 / £3.10
Flat white £2.50

MAP REF. 134

 COFFEE 3.75 / 5  **OVERALL** 4.00 / 5 ★★★★

Browns of Brockley

5 Coulgate Street, SE4 2RW

Browns of Brockley is top dog for coffee in South London. Well-trained staff pull shots on an impressive Victoria Arduino Black Eagle machine, and offer single origins on filter. The simple layout and natural colour scheme create a calming atmosphere. Owner Ross Brown is committed to sourcing the highest quality ingredients for both coffee and food. Local suppliers include Flock & Herd butchers and Blackwood Cheese, whilst Northiam Dairy supplies deliciously sweet milk. The friendly team is completed by Ludd the pug, Browns' lovable canine mascot.

+44(0)20 8692 0722
www.brownsofbrockley.com
⊖ Brockley

MON-FRI. 7:30am – 3:00pm
SAT. 9:00am – 5:00pm
SUN. 10:00am – 4:00pm

First opened 2009
Roaster Square Mile Coffee Roasters
Machine Victoria Arduino Black Eagle VA388, 3 groups
Grinder Mazzer Robur E, Nuova Simonelli Mythos

Espresso £2.00
Cappuccino £3.00
Latte £3.20
Flat white £3.00 — MAP REF. 135

  COFFEE 4.50 / 5 —  OVERALL 4.50 / 5 ★★★★⯨

Café Viva

44 Choumert Road, SE15 4SE

Choumert Road is a true microcosm of South East London. Café Viva squeezes between tranquil Victorian terraces and the colourful mêlée of Rye Lane's African food shops. Volcano Coffee is lovingly served in 70s cups, and tea brewed in owner Lily's collection of Brown Betty teapots. Herself a Goldsmiths College graduate, Lily hosts pieces from local artists, alongside framed messages from Peckham's post-riot 'Peace Wall'. At Café Viva terrific coffee and a strong sense of community go hand in hand.

+44(0)7918 653 533
www.cafeviva.co.uk
⊖ Peckham Rye

MON. Closed
TUE-FRI. 7:30am – 5:00pm
SAT-SUN. 9:00am – 5:00pm

First opened 2012
Roaster Volcano Coffee Works
Machine La Marzocco Linea, 2 groups
Grinder Mazzer Super Jolly

Espresso £1.80
Cappuccino £2.50
Latte £2.50
Flat white £2.50

MAP REF. 136

 COFFEE 4.00 / 5 OVERALL 4.25 / 5 ★★★★

The Coffee House by The Gentlemen Baristas

63 Union Street, SE1 1SG

Lords, ladies, barons, countesses and members of the general public can expect a cordial welcome at the splendid premises of 63 Union Street. The building itself boasts a fascinating history; it originally housed one of London's oldest coffee roasteries dating back to the 18th century. Proprietors Henry Ayers and Edward Parkes, two tweed-clad coffee chaps, plan to reinstate roasting on the site later in 2015. The coffee here is really rather spiffing, but owners of particularly dashing moustaches should exercise caution when indulging in cappuccinos.

+44(0)7817 350 067
www.thegentlemenbaristas.com
⊖ Borough / London Bridge

MON-FRI. 7:30am - 6:00pm
SAT. 8:30am - 5:00pm
SUN. 10:00 - 4:00pm

First opened 2014
Roaster House roast and Campbell & Syme
Machine La Marzocco Linea, 3 groups
Grinder Mazzer Major x3, Mazzer Mini

Espresso £1.50 / £2.00
Cappuccino £2.50
Latte £2.50 / £2.70
Flat white £2.50

MAP REF.

COFFEE
4.25 / 5

OVERALL
4.25 / 5 ★★★★☆

Daily Goods

36 Camberwell Church Street, SE5 8QZ

Relocating from the concession at Kinoko Cycles, Daily Goods is a much needed shot in the arm for Camberwell's café scene. Run by Carter Donnell, who practised his craft at New York's renowned Ninth Street Espresso, Daily Goods has a relaxed atmosphere attracting a cross-section of Camberwell residents. In a doff of the (baseball) cap to Yankee coffee culture, the menu includes filter coffee served in American diner-style mugs. But forget any preconceptions you might have about bulk brew; the baristas at Daily Goods are anything but casual about their coffee.

www.dailygoodslondon.co.uk
⊖ Denmark Hill

MON-FRI. 7:30am – 6:30pm
SAT. 9:30am – 5:30pm
SUN. 10:00am – 5:00pm

First opened 2014
Roaster Workshop Coffee Co.
Machine La Marzocco Linea, 2 groups
Grinder Mazzer Super Jolly, Anfim, Ditting

Espresso £2.00
Cappuccino £2.80
Latte £2.80
Flat white £2.60

MAP REF. 138

COFFEE
4.50 / 5

OVERALL
4.25 / 5
★★★★½

Fee & Brown

50 High Street, Beckenham, BR3 1AY

Fee & Brown sets a new benchmark for coffee in London's suburbs. Husband and wife team Ercan and Del serve a Caravan blend custom-roasted to their specifications. The artisan lunch menu, ample space, and plentiful seating make Fee & Brown an excellent choice for groups. Baked treats fill the counter top, and whole cakes are available to order. The café's dedication to quality coffee is resolutely upheld by the team of passionate young baristas.

+44(0)20 8658 1996
www.feeandbrown.com
Beckenham Junction Rail

MON-FRI. 7:30am – 5:00pm
SAT. 9:00am – 5:00pm
SUN. 10:00am – 4:00pm

First opened 2012
Roaster Caravan bespoke blend
Machine La Marzocco Linea, 3 groups
Grinder Mazzer Robur, Mazzer Super Jolly

Espresso £2.20
Cappuccino £2.40
Latte £2.40
Flat white £2.40

MAP REF. **139**

COFFEE
4.25 / 5

OVERALL
4.50 / 5 ★★★★✫

Four Corners Cafe

12 Lower Marsh, SE1 7RJ

Four Corners is a bright, quirky café decorated with posters bearing punchy coffee-related puns and littered with travel magazines and paraphernalia. Owner Gary Baxter's vision puts it as a crossroads, halfway between a coffee shop and hostel, a place for people who are coming, going, or just dreaming of their next big adventure. While you plan your travels, whether to Sydenham or Sydney, enjoy a coffee made with Ozone beans, pulled on a La Marzocco Linea, and a buttery, to-die-for Balthazar pastry.

+44(0)20 8617 9591
www.four-corners-cafe.com
⊖ Waterloo / Lambeth North

MON-FRI. 7:30am - 6:30pm
SAT. 9:00am - 5:00pm
SUN. Closed

First opened 2013
Roaster Ozone Coffee Roasters
Machine La Marzocco Linea, 2 groups
Grinder Mazzer Major

Espresso £2.00
Cappuccino £2.50
Latte £2.60
Flat white £2.50

MAP REF. **140**

COFFEE 4.00 / 5	OVERALL 4.25 / 5
🫘🫘🫘🫘🫘	★★★★✩

Fowlds Cafe

3 Addington Square, SE5 7JZ

Tucked away on bohemian Addington Square, this charming little café is a collaboration with Fowlds upholstery firm, occupying the site since 1926. This family business continues to operate from the rear of the property, while the shopfront is given over to coffee and cake. The workshop itself is occasionally repurposed for atmospheric candle-lit supper clubs. Fowlds' beautiful old-fashioned shop sign hangs from the facade, casting an enchanting spell over this forgotten corner of Camberwell. Fowlds is a quietly brilliant coffee spot well worth a detour to visit.

+44(0)20 3417 4500
Oval / Kennington

MON–WED. 7:30am – 5:00pm
THU. 7:30am – 10:30pm
SAT. 8:30am – 5:00pm
SUN. 9:30am – 4:00pm

First opened 2014
Roaster Square Mile Coffee Roasters
Machine La Marzocco Linea, 2 groups
Grinder Anfim

Espresso £2.00
Cappuccino £2.50
Latte £2.50
Flat white £2.50

MAP REF. **141**

 COFFEE 4.00 / 5   **OVERALL** 4.25 / 5

General Store

174 Bellenden Road, SE15 4BW

General Store is one of a rare breed of delicatessen with a real understanding of speciality coffee. Workshop espresso is pulled from a La Marzocco, and an assortment of the Clerkenwell roaster's beans are available whole or ground to order. The owners' passion for quality food and drink is abundantly clear in the irresistible range of provisions filling the shelves: fresh fruit and vegetables, dry goods, cured meats and cheeses. All produce is selected with an exceptionally keen eye for provenance and seasonality. Complement your coffee with an epic pastry sourced from Little Bread Pedlar bakery.

+44(0)20 7642 2129
www.generalsto.re
⊖ Peckham Rye

MON-TUE. Closed
WED-FRI. 9:00am - 7:00pm
SAT. 9:00am - 5:00pm
SUN. 10:00am - 4:00pm

First opened 2013
Roaster Workshop Coffee Co.
Machine La Marzocco Linea, 2 groups
Grinder Mazzer Super Jolly

Espresso £2.00
Cappuccino £2.60
Latte £2.60
Flat white £2.60

MAP REF. 142

COFFEE 4.25 / 5	OVERALL 4.25 / 5

155

Monmouth Coffee Company Borough

2 Park Street, SE1 9AB

Monmouth Coffee Company has developed a cult-like following among many Londoners who make weekly pilgrimages to this coffee mecca. The Borough Market venue, larger than the Covent Garden premises, is incredibly popular with market regulars and tourists, and is appropriately surrounded by some of the city's finest producers of foods and beverages. Fridays and Saturdays are extremely busy, so a weekday trip is a safer bet. Also worth a visit is Monmouth's Bermondsey outpost, at Arch 3 Spa North, open Saturdays only 9:00am – 1:30pm.

+44(0)20 7232 3010
www.monmouthcoffee.co.uk
London Bridge

Sister locations Covent Garden / Bermondsey

MON–SAT. 7:30am – 6:00pm
SUN. Closed

First opened 2001
Roaster Monmouth Coffee Company
Machine La Marzocco Linea, 2 groups x2
Grinder Mazzer Robur x2

Espresso £1.50
Cappuccino £2.50
Latte £2.50
Flat white £2.50

MAP REF.

    COFFEE 4.50 / 5  OVERALL 4.50 / 5 ★★★★⯪

No67 at South London Gallery

67 Peckham Road, SE5 8UH

Set within a handsome townhouse adjoining the South London Gallery, No67 is a popular café and dining room frequently packed out for weekend brunch. At less busy periods it offers a soothing respite from the din of busy Camberwell. The chocolaty Allpress coffee is handled well, and makes an excellent complement to the outstanding Full Spanglish breakfast. Open well into the evening, No67 is also an ideal spot to enjoy great wine, cocktails and craft beer with the cultured South London crowd.

+44(0)20 7252 7649
www.number67.co.uk
⊖ Peckham Rye / Denmark Hill

MON. Closed
TUE. 8:00am – 6:30pm
WED-FRI. 8:00am – 11:00pm
SAT. 10:00am – 11:00pm
SUN. 10:00am – 6:30pm

First opened 2010
Roaster Allpress Espresso
Machine La Marzocco FB/80, 2 groups
Grinder Mazzer Robur, Mazzer Super Jolly

Espresso £1.30 / £1.80
Cappuccino £2.30 / £2.80
Latte £2.30 / £2.80
Flat white £2.30 / £2.80

MAP REF. 144

COFFEE 4.25 / 5

OVERALL 4.25 / 5 ★★★★⯪

ScooterCaffè

132 Lower Marsh, SE1 7AE

The brainchild of New Zealand ex-aircraft engineer Craig O'Dwyer, ScooterCaffè started life as a Vespa workshop. However, O'Dwyer soon branched out into coffee and now his collection of vintage machinery and scooter memorabilia adorns a truly unique café space. The moody basement area hosts movie, music and comedy nights. Coffee is made on a beautiful 1960s espresso machine, accompanied by vintage grinders. ScooterCaffè is one of London's most unique retro coffee experiences.

+44(0)20 7620 1421
⊖ Lambeth North / Waterloo

Sister locations Cable Café

MON-THU. 8:30am – 11:00pm
FRI. 8:30am – 12:00am
SAT. 10:00am – 12:00am
SUN. 10:00am – 11:00pm

First opened 2009
Roaster ScooterCaffè bespoke blend
Machine 1965 Gaggia, 3 groups
Grinder La San Marco

Espresso £1.80
Cappuccino £2.30
Latte £2.30
Flat white £2.30

MAP REF.

 COFFEE 3.75 / 5 OVERALL 4.00 / 5 ★★★★☆

Small White Elephant

28 Choumert Road, SE15 4SE

For those days when you're furious with the world, we prescribe a trip to Small White Elephant. This café is a calming sanctuary run by Dale Carney and Jen Richardson, two of the nicest people ever to open a coffee shop. Let us count the ways they will make you smile: local art on the walls, a book exchange, a veritable jungle of plants, tasty Alchemy coffee and a even a monthly jazz night. We must also mention the French toast. This is the real deal; triumphant eggy slabs saturated in syrup. Whatever your day has thrown at you, Small White Elephant has a remedy.

www.smallwhiteelephant.com
 Peckham Rye

MON. 9:00am – 6:00pm
TUE. Closed
WED-FRI. 9:00am – 6:00pm
SAT-SUN. 10:00am – 5:30pm

First opened 2014
Roaster Alchemy, Extract Coffee Roasters
Machine La Marzocco Linea, 3 groups
Grinder Mazzer Super Jolly

Espresso £1.90
Cappuccino £2.40
Latte £2.50
Flat white £2.40

MAP REF. 146

COFFEE 4.25 / 5   **OVERALL** 4.25 / 5 ★★★★½

St. David Coffee House

5 David's Road, SE23 3EP

St. David Coffee House brims with retro charm. Local artists, actors, musicians and families come here in droves to sip espresso among the books, stacks of vinyl, and vintage movie memorabilia. The owners host regular events, such as pizza nights in collaboration with sourdough pizza purveyors Van Dough. This isn't a café which is trying hard to be liked; the atmosphere feels welcoming and uncontrived. Its easy-going nature and strong community links have made it very much part of Forest Hill life.

+44(0)20 8291 6646
www.stdavidcoffeehouse.co.uk
 Forest Hill

MON. Closed
TUE-FRI. 8:00am – 5:00pm
SAT. 9:00am – 6:00pm
SUN. 10:00am – 4:00pm

First opened 2010
Roaster Square Mile Coffee Roasters and guests
Machine Rancilio Classe 10, 2 groups
Grinder Anfim

Espresso £1.80
Cappuccino £2.40
Latte £2.40
Flat white £2.30

MAP REF. 147

COFFEE 4.00 / 5   **OVERALL** 4.00 / 5 ★★★★☆

Volcano Coffee House

Parkhall Trading Estate, 40 Martell Road, SE21 8EN

Photo courtesy of the venue

Volcano operates from a former electronics factory, surprisingly located among a row of terraced houses. This architecturally impressive building houses the roastery, and a spacious café. Opt for Volcano's own 'Fullsteam' espresso blend, or try a range of single estate filters. A collection of antique coffee machines and a vintage roaster displayed on gallery-style plinths announce the founders' shared love for classic machinery. Volcano resonates with a deep passion for espresso culture, past and present.

+44(0)20 8761 8415
www.volcanocoffeeworks.com
West Norwood Rail / West Dulwich Rail

MON–FRI. 8:00am – 4:30pm
SAT. 9:00am – 4:30pm
SUN. Closed

First opened 2012
Roaster Volcano Coffee Works
Machine La Marzocco Linea, 2 groups
Grinder Mazzer Major, Mazzer Super Jolly

Espresso £2.00
Cappuccino £2.20
Latte £2.20
Flat white £2.20

MAP REF. 148

COFFEE 4.75 / 5

OVERALL 4.50 / 5

The Watch House

199 Bermondsey Street, SE1 3UW

During the nineteenth century, the fascinating Watch House building housed guards protecting the churchyard of St Mary Magdalen against body snatchers. This unique octagonal space has been transformed into a cosy retreat complete with rustic wooden lampshades, underfloor heating and even a wood-burning hearth. Thankfully The Watch House doesn't disappoint Bermondsey Street's discerning foodies. In addition to hand-roasted Ozone coffee, the counter is stacked high with homemade sandwiches, and the platters piled deep with doughnuts sourced from famed St John Bakery.

+44(0)20 7407 5431
www.watchhousecoffee.com
⊖ London Bridge

MON–FRI. 7:00am – 6:00pm
SAT. 8:00am – 6:00pm
SUN. 9:00am – 6:00pm

First opened 2014
Roaster Ozone Coffee Roasters
Machine La Marzocco Linea PB, 2 groups
Grinder Mazzer Major, Mahlkönig EK 43

Espresso £1.90 / £2.00
Cappuccino £2.40 / £2.70
Latte £2.30 / £2.60
Flat white £2.20

MAP REF. 149

COFFEE 4.00 / 5		OVERALL 4.25 / 5	★★★★⯪

With Jam and Bread

386 Lee High Road, SE12 8RW

With Jam and Bread is a cheerful café in which you could happily spend an entire afternoon. Passionate owner Jennie Milsom is also a food and drink writer. This child-friendly venue combines the best elements of a homely neighbourhood retreat with coffee of a standard rarely encountered in London's suburban belt. Delicious lunch and cake options are also available. Occupying the site of a former art gallery, With Jam and Bread retains an exhibition space towards the rear.

+44(0)20 8318 4040
www.withjamandbread.com
⇌ Lee Rail / Hither Green Rail

MON–FRI. 8:00am – 3:00pm
SAT. 9:30am – 4:00pm
SUN. Closed

First opened 2011
Roaster Volcano Coffee Works
Machine La Marzocco Linea, 2 groups
Grinder Anfim, Mazzer Super Jolly

Espresso £1.90
Cappuccino £2.70
Latte £2.70
Flat white £2.60

MAP REF. 150

COFFEE 4.00 / 5		OVERALL 4.25 / 5	★★★★⯪

South West

South West London contains a dizzying array of cultural influences, from the Afro-Caribbean heritage of Brixton to the antipodean-influenced lifestyle of Clapham and the genteel suburban rhythms of Putney. The area's colourful and creative coffee culture reflects these unique influences and local quirks.

Artisan Putney

203 Upper Richmond Road, Putney, SW15 6SG

Photo courtesy of the venue

Artisan's motto "Obsessively passionate about coffee" is an apt philosophy for this busy café. The Putney site and its sister venues benefit from advanced water filtration systems and serve beautiful single origin coffees from guest roasters. The warm, light-filled space is furnished with quirky furniture, and the inventive loyalty scheme encourages customers to spin a 'wheel of fortune' to determine their reward. Everyone from mums with prams to picky coffee geeks will be met by a genuinely warm welcome and superb coffee.

+44(0)20 8617 3477
www.artisancoffee.co.uk
◉ East Putney / ⇌ Putney Rail

Sister locations Ealing / Stamford Brook

MON–FRI. 7:00am - 6:00pm
SAT. 8:00am - 6:00pm
SUN. 8:30am - 6:00pm

First opened 2011
Roaster Allpress Espresso
Machine La Marzocco FB/80, 3 groups
Grinder Mazzer Robur, Mazzer Super Jolly, Mahlkönig Tanzania

Espresso £2.00
Cappuccino £2.40 / £2.70
Latte £2.40 / £2.70
Flat white £2.40 / £2.70

MAP REF. **151**

COFFEE 4.50 / 5   **OVERALL** 4.50 / 5 ★★★★✦

Birdhouse

123 St John's Hill, SW11 1SZ

This perfectly formed café is a striking addition to St John's Hill. The interior is light, beautifully furnished in brushed steel and vintage wood, punctuated with splashes of bright yellow. Bird images and other avian touches create a unique experience, and an old carpenter's work block serves a new duty as a coffee bar. At weekends Birdhouse is a flurry of activity as plates of steaming baked eggs and beautifully-poured flat whites make their way to brunching Battersea locals.

+44(0)20 7228 6663
www.birdhou.se
⊖ Clapham Junction

MON-FRI. 7:00am – 4:00pm
SAT-SUN. 9:00am – 5:00pm

First opened 2011
Roaster Climpson & Sons
Machine La Marzocco Linea, 3 groups
Grinder Anfim, Mazzer Robur E

Espresso £2.00
Cappuccino £2.50 / £2.80
Latte £2.50 / £2.80
Flat white £2.50

MAP REF. 152

COFFEE 4.25 / 5	OVERALL 4.25 / 5
🫘🫘🫘🫘🫘	★★★★⯪

The Black Lab Coffee House

18 Clapham Common Southside, SW4 7AB

Photo courtesy of the venue

The Black Lab Coffee House is a warm and cosy choice in an area surprisingly light on good cafés. The recently refurbished venue with comfortable seating is a great place to catch up with friends, but can fill up rapidly at weekends. Black Lab has upped its coffee game with a move to Alchemy coffee, and now offers a range of home brewing gear and beans ground to order. Single estate coffees brewed by AeroPress are also offered at less busy periods.

+44(0)20 7738 8441
www.blacklabcoffee.com
⊖ Clapham Common

MON-FRI. 7:30am – 5:30pm
SAT-SUN. 9:00am – 5:00pm

First opened 2010
Roaster Alchemy
Machine La Marzocco Linea, 2 groups
Grinder Mahlkönig K 30, Mazzer Kony x 2, Mahlkönig EK 43

Espresso £1.80
Cappuccino £2.50
Latte £2.60
Flat white £2.40

MAP REF. 153

COFFEE 4.25 / 5   OVERALL 4.25 / 5 ★★★★☆

Brew Battersea

45 Northcote Road, SW11 1NJ

A favourite with the Northcote Road set, Brew is a cheerful antidote to the many chain coffee stores nearby. Simple and cosy, Brew offers a comprehensive menu in a breezy, laidback environment. However, this café is best known for its sensational breakfasts, which feature only the best quality local ingredients, as well as juices and smoothies. A tantalising beer and wine list is also on offer.

+44(0)20 7585 2198
www.brew-cafe.com
⊖ Clapham Junction

Sister locations Wimbledon / Putney / Battersea

MON-SAT. 7:00am - 6:00pm
SUN. 8:00am - 6:00pm

First opened 2008
Roaster Allpress Espresso
Machine La Marzocco Linea, 2 groups
Grinder Mazzer Super Jolly

Espresso £2.30 / £2.60
Cappuccino £2.90
Latte £2.90
Flat white £2.90

MAP REF. 154

COFFEE **4.00 / 5** 🫘🫘🫘🫘🫘

OVERALL **4.25 / 5** ★★★★✬

Brickwood

16 Clapham Common South Side, SW4 7AB

Brickwood brings proper Aussie-style coffee and brunches to Clapham. Corn fritters with a choice of halloumi and poached egg, or avocado and chorizo ought to sort you out after a heavy Friday night. With an outdoor courtyard at the rear, visitors can enjoy their sunny Antipodean brunch under a (hopefully!) bright English sky. The punchy Caravan coffee perfectly complements the food's bold flavours, and is confidently prepared by enthusiastic baristas on a stunning mint green La Marzocco, affectionately nicknamed 'Lola'.

+44(0)20 7819 9614
www.brickwoodlondon.com
⊖ Clapham Common

MON–FRI. 7:00am – 6:00pm
SAT–SUN. 9:00am – 6:00pm

First opened 2013
Roaster Caravan and guests
Machine La Marzocco FB/80, 2 groups
Grinder Mazzer Major, Mazzer Jolly

Espresso £2.30
Cappuccino £2.50
Latte £2.50
Flat white £2.50

MAP REF. 155

| COFFEE 4.25 / 5 |  | OVERALL 4.50 / 5 | ★★★★✩ |

Federation Coffee

Unit 77-78 Brixton Village Market, Coldharbour Lane, SW9 8PS

Federation has led a flourishing of foodie culture in the rapidly developing Brixton Village Market, and is surrounded by a host of other cafés and restaurants following its lead. The seating arrayed around the outside of the café affords a prime position to people-watch and soak up the lively atmosphere of the covered market. Now under the management of Joe Cannon & Nick Balfe (owners of the highly regarded Brixton restaurant, Salon), Federation offers a small but high quality food menu and plans to introduce a brew bar in the near future.

www.federationcoffee.com
⊖ Brixton

Sister locations Brighton Terrace
Takeaway Hatch

MON–FRI. 8:00am – 5:00pm
SAT. 9:00am – 6:00pm
SUN. 9:00am – 5:00pm

First opened 2010
Roaster Campbell & Syme
Machine Synesso Cyncra, 3 groups
Grinder Mazzer Robur, Anfim

Espresso £2.00
Cappuccino £2.60
Latte £2.60
Flat white £2.60

MAP REF. 156

| COFFEE 4.50 / 5 | | OVERALL 4.50 / 5 | ★★★★✩ |

Fields

2 Rookery Road, Clapham Common, SW4 9DD

At first glance, Fields appears about as promising a foodie destination as a chip van on an industrial estate. But once inside the squat building situated next to Clapham's skatepark, you soon realise that this is a completely different kettle of fish. Opened by the team behind M1lk, Fields has a clean, functional aesthetic with an emphasis on creative cooking and exceptional coffee. The inspired brunch menu includes the likes of poached eggs with espresso-infused hollandaise sauce. Benefitting from plenty of outdoor seating, Fields really comes into its own in the summer months.

+44(0)20 8772 9085
www.fieldscafe.com
⊖ Clapham Common

Sister locations M1lk

MON-SUN. 9:00am – 5:00pm

First opened 2014
Roaster Workshop Coffee Co., Koppi
Machine Kees van der Westen Spirit, 3 groups
Grinder Mazzer Robur E, Mahlkönig EK 43

Espresso £2.00
Cappuccino £2.50
Latte £2.50
Flat white £2.40

MAP REF. 157

COFFEE 4.50 / 5	OVERALL 4.50 / 5

Grind Coffee Bar Putney

79 Lower Richmond Road, SW15 1ET

This stylish, contemporary café was one of the pioneers on the thriving Putney coffee scene. Grind's friendly antipodean atmosphere and excellent flat whites make it popular with local ex-pats, but the use of British ingredients give it a decidedly local outlook. In summer 2014, Grind launched Grind Roast Works, supplying its two sites with single origin roasts and the chocolaty Caveman espresso blend. The café's corner location and tempting range of homemade cakes and savouries make it difficult to pass without popping in for a coffee and a chat with the genial team of baristas.

+44(0)20 8789 5101
www.grindcoffeebar.co.uk
⊖ Putney Bridge

Sister locations Westfield Stratford City

MON–FRI. 7:00am – 6:00pm
SAT–SUN. 8:00am –6:00pm

First opened 2010
Roaster Grind Roast Works
Machine La Marzocco Strada, 3 groups
Grinder Mazzer Robur E x2

Espresso £1.80
Cappuccino £2.30 / £2.70
Latte £2.30 / £2.70
Flat white £2.30 / £2.70

MAP REF.

 **COFFEE** 4.50 / 5  **OVERALL** 4.25 / 5 ★★★★✦

La Moka

141 Battersea High Street, SW11 3JS

La Moka is tiny but irresistible. It's the sort of café you feel you ought to tell your friends about, but decide not to so you can have it all to yourself. Owners Ni and Ettore Moraschinelli have somehow managed to cheat the laws of physics to fit so many good things into such a pint-sized space. Ni, a pastry chef by training, sources a delectable selection of cakes, pastries and breads. Every aspect of the café is beautifully visualised courtesy of Ettore's graphic design skills. On Saturdays, a farmers' market arrives on the street outside, fuelled by community spirit and La Moka's revitalising coffee.

+44(0)20 3663 8802
www.lamoka.co.uk
⊖ Clapham Junction

MON–SAT. 6:00am – 5:30pm
SUN. 9:00am – 4:00pm

First opened 2014
Roaster Allpress Espresso
Machine La Marzocco FB/80, 2 groups
Grinder Mazzer Robur, Mazzer Super Jolly

Espresso £1.50 / £1.70
Cappuccino £2.50 / £2.70
Latte £2.50 / £2.70
Flat white £2.40

MAP REF. 159

COFFEE 4.25 / 5	OVERALL 4.25 / 5

The Lido Cafe

Brockwell Lido, Dulwich Road, SE24 0PA

A bracing dip in Brockwell Lido is guaranteed to wake you up in the morning (just as effectively as a double espresso!) Thankfully, you don't need to take the plunge to enjoy the hospitality at The Lido Cafe. In summer, the palm-shaded terrace overlooking the pool is a special spot to sip flat whites, or even indulge in a Prosecco brunch. Open for breakfast, lunch or dinner all year round, this Art Deco retreat is a truly unique addition to London's café culture.

+44(0)20 7737 8183
www.thelidocafe.co.uk
≥ Herne Hill Rail

MON-TUE. 9:00am - 5:00pm
WED-SAT. 9:00am - 11:00pm
SUN. 9:00am - 5:00pm

First opened 2009
Roaster Allpress Espresso
Machine La Marzocco FB/80, 3 groups
Grinder Mazzer Robur

Espresso £1.90
Cappuccino £2.60
Latte £2.60
Flat white £2.50

MAP REF.

COFFEE	OVERALL
4.25 / 5	4.25 / 5

M1lk

20 Bedford Hill, SW12 9RG

M1lk is a magnificent medley of artisan coffee and Aussie-style food, with a sprinkling of British eccentricity. The playful and nostalgic theme borders on the bizarre with the café's baby head motif. The hip team take their espresso very seriously, squeezing every drop of performance from their La Marzocco Linea. Alternatively, try an AeroPress to appreciate the subtleties of the single origins on offer. Cupping classes are also available for those interested in developing their own coffee expertise.

+44(0)20 8772 9085
www.m1lk.co.uk
⊖ Balham

Sister locations Fields

MON-SAT. 8:00am - 5:00pm
SUN. 9:00am - 5:00pm

First opened 2012
Roaster Workshop Coffee Co, Koppi
Machine La Marzocco Linea, 2 groups
Grinder Anfim, Mazzer Robur E, Mahlkönig EK 43

Espresso £2.00
Cappuccino £2.40
Latte £2.50
Flat white £2.40

MAP REF.

COFFEE	OVERALL
4.50 / 5	4.25 / 5

Story Coffee

115 St John's Hill, SW11 1SZ

Story Coffee rather belongs to a different world. A world where a person's golden time isn't bullied by smartphones, menial tasks or wailing offspring. A world where delicious things are handed to them across the counter. A world where a beautifully-poured coffee has the power to unscramble the scrambled. Floods of light, blonde wood, fresh flowers on the tables, charming owners and an impeccable list of suppliers: it's all there. Like a great novel, Story transports you to an altogether better place.

www.storycoffee.co.uk
⊖ Clapham Junction

MON-FRI. 7:00am – 4:00pm
SAT-SUN. 9:00am – 5:00pm

First opened 2014
Roaster Square Mile Coffee Roasters and guests
Machine Kees van der Western Spirit, 2 groups
Grinder Nuova Simonelli Mythos, Mahlkönig EK 43

Espresso £2.00
Cappuccino £2.60
Latte £2.60
Flat white £2.60

MAP REF. 162

COFFEE 4.50 / 5	OVERALL 4.50 / 5

Tamp

1 Devonshire Road, W4 2EU

Nestled between the chi chi boutiques of Devonshire Road, Tamp resembles a rustic lodge with its wood-clad floor, ceiling and bar. The owner's dog, ensconced in its bed at the rear of the store, completes the homely scene. This isn't just a destination to put your feet up, though. Tamp offers coffee from up-and-coming Mission Coffee Works and guest beans from respected roasters including Berlin's The Barn. Even the non-homogenised milk has been carefully sourced from West Sussex's Goodwood Estate, making deliciously sweet and creamy cappuccinos.

www.tampcoffee.co.uk
⊖ Turnham Green

MON-FRI. 8:00am - 5:30pm
SAT. 8:00am - 6:00pm
SUN. 9:00am - 5:30pm

First opened 2014
Roaster Mission Coffee Works
Machine La Marzocco GB/5, 3 groups
Grinder Nuova Simonelli Mythos, Mahlkönig K 30, Mahlkönig EK 43

Espresso £2.20
Cappuccino £2.60
Latte £2.60
Flat white £2.60

MAP REF.

COFFEE 4.25 / 5

OVERALL 4.25 / 5 ★★★★⯪

Tried & True

279 Upper Richmond Road, SW15 6SP

Tried & True brings the best of Kiwi café culture to suburban Putney. The vibe is relaxed and welcoming. The interior eschews voguish shabby chic in favour of a bright, clean and refreshingly modern aesthetic. The baristas pull shots with utmost care, constantly re-calibrating the equipment to keep the Square Mile coffee spot on. A beautiful garden beckons in the summer months, and the delectable brunch menu has few rivals. Tried & True is one of a rare breed of top-class neighbourhood cafés.

+44(0)20 8789 0410
www.triedandtruecafe.co.uk
⊖ Putney

MON–FRI. 8:00am – 4:00pm
SAT–SUN. 8:30am – 4:30pm

First opened 2012
Roaster Square Mile Coffee Roasters
Machine La Marzocco FB/80, 3 groups
Grinder Mazzer Robur E, Mazzer Super Jolly

Espresso £2.20
Cappuccino £2.60
Latte £2.80
Flat white £2.60

MAP REF. **164**

COFFEE 4.25 / 5	🫘🫘🫘🫘🫘	OVERALL 4.25 / 5	★★★★✭

West

Home to some of London's wealthiest residents, world-renowned museums and lavish department stores, West London has a well established café culture. The number of quality-focussed coffee bars has grown in recent months, but still has a long way to go to match other London neighbourhoods.

Antipode

28 Fulham Palace Road, W6 9PH

Australians may have afflicted us with Vegemite and Mel Gibson, but when it comes to coffee and brunch, we must concede they have something to be proud of. Antipode embodies the Australian café culture Londoners have grown to adore: velvety 'flatties', delicious smashed avocado on sourdough, and disarmingly casual service. In the evening Antipode whips out a selection of Australian craft beers and wines, with negronis thrown in for good measure. Despite hunkering in the shadow of the Hammersmith flyover, hang out here and you could just as easily be in sunny Melbourne.

+44(0)20 8741 7525

⊖ Hammersmith

MON–WED. 7:00am – 6:00pm
THU. 7:00am – 9:00pm
FRI. 7:00am – 10:00pm
SAT. 8:00am – 10:00pm
SUN. 9:00am – 4:00pm

First opened 2014
Roaster Nude Espresso
Machine Nuova Simonelli Aurelia, 3 groups
Grinder Nuova Simonelli Mythos,
Mazzer Super Jolly

Espresso £2.00
Cappuccino £2.50 / £3.00
Latte £2.50 / £3.00
Flat white £2.70 / £3.20

MAP REF. 165

 **COFFEE** 4.25 / 5

 OVERALL 4.25 / 5 ★★★★⯪

Artisan Ealing

32 New Broadway, Ealing, W5 2XA

Most coffee entrepreneurs would be content with two successful coffee shops. Not Artisan founders, Edwin Harrison and Magda Woloszyn. Not only have they opened an impressive third site, they have also launched a coffee school. Connected to the main café space, the school runs home brewing masterclasses and professional SCAE-accredited qualifications. The Artisan team's enthusiasm is infectious; baristas and trainers alike are eager to surprise customers with superb guest coffees and constantly challenge themselves to push the quality bar in pursuit of coffee excellence.

+44(0)20 7998 3450
www.artisancoffee.co.uk
⊖ Ealing Broadway

Sister locations Putney / Stamford Brook

MON-FRI. 7:30am - 5:30pm
SAT-SUN. 8:30am - 5:30pm

First opened 2014
Roaster Allpress Espresso, Nude Espresso
Machine La Marzocco FB/80, 3 groups
Grinder Mazzer Kold, Mazzer Robur, Mahlkönig Tanzania

Espresso £2.00
Cappuccino £2.40 / £2.70
Latte £2.40 / £2.70
Flat white £2.40 / £2.70

MAP REF.

COFFEE 4.75 / 5	OVERALL 4.50 / 5

179

Artisan Stamford Brook

372 King Street, W6 0RX

Owners Edwin and Magda's passion for coffee began with a trip to origin, where they contributed to development work with coffee farmers. Artisan's London cafés do justice to the work of growers and roasters by diligently extracting every last drop of goodness. The interior's electric blue walls contrast magnificently with the copper counter and stools, creating a striking environment in which to enjoy the finished product. Upholding their reputation for coffee excellence, the team run coffee brewing masterclasses for customers.

+44(0)20 3302 1434
www.artisancoffee.co.uk
⊖ Stamford Brook

Sister locations Ealing / Putney

MON-FRI. 7:30am - 6:00pm
SAT. 8:00am - 6:00pm
SUN. 8:30am - 6:00pm

First opened 2013
Roaster Allpress Espresso
Machine La Marzocco FB/80, 3 groups
Grinder Mazzer Robur, Mazzer Super Jolly, Mahlkönig Tanzania

Espresso £1.50 / £1.90
Cappuccino £2.20 / £2.50
Latte £2.20 / £2.50
Flat white £2.20 / £2.50

MAP REF. 167

| COFFEE 4.50 / 5 | | OVERALL 4.50 / 5 | ★ ★ ★ ★ ⯪ |

Cable Co.

4 Bridge House, Chamberlayne Road, NW10 3NR

 NEW

After years in the coffee wilderness, Kensal Rise finally has speciality coffee courtesy of Cable Co. The spartan interior of this unassuming coffee bar follows a factory theme: concrete, raw timber and black tiling contrast with copper lamp shades which provide welcome flashes of colour. An oil drum repurposed as a sugar station completes the industrial atmosphere. Aromatic Climpson & Sons coffee is complemented by a small selection of toasties and a tempting range of cakes, including irresistible blueberry crumble loaf cake.

+44(0)7707 626 651
⊖ Kensal Rise

Sister locations Wired 194

MON-FRI. 7:30am - 5:00pm
SAT-SUN. 9:00am - 5:00pm

First opened 2014
Roaster Climpson & Sons
Machine La Marzocco FB/70, 3 groups
Grinder Mazzer Major, Mazzer Super Jolly, Mazzer Mini

Espresso £2.00
Cappuccino £2.50
Latte £2.50
Flat white £2.40

MAP REF. 168

| COFFEE 4.00 / 5 |  | OVERALL 4.00 / 5 | ★ ★ ★ ★ ☆ |

Chairs and Coffee

512 Fulham Road, SW6 5NJ

Chairs and Coffee is the labour of two friends, Simone Guerini Rocco and Roberto D'alessandro. The duo's passion emanates from every facet of the café: their Italian pride pours from the vintage Faema espresso machine (rescued from a priest's basement); their ingenuity whirrs in the restored 1950s roaster; the free Friday night buffets declare their love of hospitality; and the chairs casually suspended from the ceiling (because they like "being ridiculous") embody their unbridled eccentricity. Truly authentic cafés like Chairs and Coffee are a rarity; this is one to be cherished.

+44(0)20 7018 1913
www.chairsandcoffee.co.uk
 Fulham Broadway

MON. Closed
TUE-FRI. 8:00am - 11:00pm
SAT. 9:00am - 11:00pm
SUN. 9:00am - 6:00pm

First opened 2013
Roaster Union Hand-Roasted
Machine Faema E61, 2 groups
Grinder Mazzer Major x2

Espresso £1.80 / £2.00
Cappuccino £2.40
Latte £2.40
Flat white £2.40

MAP REF. 169

 **COFFEE** 4.25 / 5 **OVERALL** 4.25 / 5

Electric Coffee Co.

40 Haven Green, Ealing, W5 2NX

Stepping inside this Ealing enclave, one's gaze is immediately stolen by the Kees van der Westen Mirage coffee machine. Crafted with aircraft-grade aluminium, this stunning machine is the supercharged dynamo of Electric Coffee Co. Piloted by an enthusiastic team, the Mirage fires out gutsy espresso roasted by Automaton. Filter coffee is also available should you prefer a more gentle take-off. Electric Coffee Co. is one of the best third wave coffee shops in the west.

+44(0)20 8991 1010
www.electriccoffee.co.uk
⊖ Ealing Broadway

MON–FRI. 7:00am – 6:00pm
SAT. 8:00am – 6:00pm
SAT. 9:00am – 6:00pm

First opened 2008
Roaster Automaton and guests
Machine Kees van der Westen Mirage Veloce, 3 groups
Grinder Mazzer Robur E x2, Anfim Super Caimano

Espresso £1.90
Cappuccino £2.60 / £2.80
Latte £2.60 / £2.80
Flat white £2.60   MAP REF. 170

 COFFEE 4.50 / 5  OVERALL 4.50 / 5 ★★★★⯪

Fernandez & Wells South Kensington

8a Exhibition Road, SW7 2HF

This Fernandez & Wells' venue is a godsend for coffee-starved West Londoners and visitors to the nearby museums. The interior's high ceiling and elegant cornicing resonate with South Kensington's noble architecture. Cured meats hang artfully against the rear wall, accompanied by a shelf of well-chosen wines. There's plenty of seating round the back, which is fortunate as you'll almost certainly want to complement your Has Bean coffee with a plate of charcuterie.

+44(0)20 7589 7473
www.fernandezandwells.com
⊖ South Kensington

Sister locations Somerset House / Denmark Street / Beak Street / Lexington Street / Duke Street

MON–FRI. 8:00am – 10:00pm
SAT. 9:00am – 10:00pm
SUN. 9:00am – 8:00pm

First opened 2012
Roaster Has Bean bespoke blend
Machine Synesso Cyncra, 3 groups
Grinder Mazzer Robur E x2, Mahlkönig Tanzania

Espresso £2.40
Cappuccino £2.80
Latte £2.80
Flat white £2.80

MAP REF. 171

COFFEE 4.25 / 5 OVERALL 4.50 / 5 ★★★★⯪

Hally's

60 New Kings Road, SW6 4LS

The vibe at Hally's is airy California cool. The reclaimed clapboard and whitewashed brick walls are punctuated by citrus yellow bar stools and neon signs. You may just be popping in for a Monmouth coffee, but be prepared to stay for longer once you catch sight of the food on offer, which includes an outstanding array of salads and a bold-flavoured brunch menu. Across the street, newly opened sister shop, Little H, offers a condensed Hally's menu including breakfast, lunch and fabulous fresh juices and smoothies.

+44(0)20 3302 7408
www.hallysparsonsgreen.com
⊖ Parsons Green

Sister locations Little H

SAT-WED. 8:00am – 6:00pm
THU-FRI. 8:00am – 11:00pm

First opened 2013
Roaster Monmouth Coffee Company
Machine La Marzocco Linea, 2 groups
Grinder Mazzer Kold

Espresso £2.00
Cappuccino £2.60 / £2.90
Latte £2.60 / £2.90
Flat white £2.60 / £2.90

MAP REF. **172**

Iris & June

1 Howick Place, SW1P 1WG

The arrival of Iris & June (named after the owner's grandparents) marks a turning point in the fortunes for the Victoria neighbourhood. The interior's concrete floors, exposed ventilation ducts and industrial tiling lend the café an air of Shoreditch cool. Upon entering, customers are greeted by a sumptuous display of salads and sandwiches behind polished glass. Iris & June feels like a keystone in this new Victoria, injecting a dose of vigour and setting a high standard for a stylish, intelligent coffee bar in an area previously bereft of speciality coffee.

+44(0)20 7828 3130
www.irisandjune.com
🚇 Victoria / St James's Park

MON-FRI. 7:30am – 5:30pm
SAT. 8:30am – 4:00pm
SUN. Closed

First opened 2014
Roaster Ozone Coffee Roasters
Machine La Marzocco Strada, 3 groups
Grinder Mazzer Robur E, Mahlkönig EK 43

Espresso £2.40
Cappuccino £2.80
Latte £2.80
Flat white £2.70

MAP REF.

 COFFEE 4.50 / 5  OVERALL 4.50 / 5 ★★★★✭

St Clements Cafe

201 New Kings Road, SW6 4SR

The menu at St Clements is so good it presents some tough decisions. Agonising choices must be made between seductive salads and tantalising tarts. Olivia Cundy, a professional chef with ten years' experience, composes marvellous plates of seasonal fare, paired with hand-roasted coffee from Ozone, one of East London's best roasteries. The café offers comfortable seating and a delightful terrace opening out to the street. Little details like bone-handled knives and tasteful teal decor lend the café an air of elegance.

+44(0)20 7998 8919
www.stclementscafe.co.uk
⊖ Parsons Green

MON–FRI. 8:00am – 5:30pm
SAT. 8:30am – 5:30pm
SUN. 9:00am – 5:30pm

First opened 2014
Roaster Ozone Coffee Roasters
Machine La Marzocco FB/80, 2 groups
Grinder Mazzer Kony, Mazzer Super Jolly

Espresso £1.90 / £2.30
Cappuccino £2.60 / £3.00
Latte £2.60 / £3.00
Flat white £2.50 / £2.80

MAP REF. **174**

COFFEE
4.00 / 5

OVERALL
4.50 / 5 ★★★★✦

Talkhouse Coffee

275 Portobello Road, W11 1LR

Photo courtesy of the venue

The minimalist decor, whitewashed walls and high ceilings lend Talkhouse a sense of calming gravitas. This impressive space near the vibrant Portobello market has rapidly established its third wave coffee credentials, employing some of London's most talented baristas and offering beans from top artisan roasters. Overseen by Latte Art Champion Miguel Lamora, the coffee is meticulously prepared and presented. When it comes to a quality brew in west London, Talkhouse is the name on everyone's lips.

+44(0)20 7221 8992
www.talkhousecoffee.com
⊖ Ladbroke Grove

MON. Closed
TUE-FRI. 8:00am – 5:00pm
SAT. 8:30am – 6:00pm
SUN. 9:30 – 5:00pm

First opened 2013
Roaster Square Mile Coffee Roasters, James Gourmet, Tate Roasters
Machine Synesso Hydra, 3 groups
Grinder Anfim Super Caimano, Mahlkönig Tanzania

Espresso £2.20 / £2.40
Cappuccino £2.70
Latte £3.00
Flat white £2.90

MAP REF. 175

COFFEE 4.75 / 5		OVERALL 4.50 / 5	

Photo: Alessandro Bonuzzi

Coffee Knowledge

Behind every cup of coffee is a unique story. On its journey from coffee tree to cup, coffee passes through the hands of a number of skilled individuals. Over the following pages, expert contributors share their specialist knowledge. As you will see, the coffee we enjoy is the result of a rich and complex process, and there is always something new to learn.

Coffee at Origin

by **Mike Riley**, Falcon Speciality Green Coffee Importers

If you go into London's vibrant coffee community today and ask any good barista what makes a perfect cup of coffee, they will always tell you that it starts with the bean. Beyond the roasting technique, the perfect grind, and exact temperatures and precision pressure of a modern espresso machine, we must look to the dedicated coffee farmer who toils away in the tropical lands of Africa, Asia and Latin America. They are the first heroes of our trade.

Approximately 25 million people in over 50 countries are involved in producing coffee. The bean, or seed to be exact, is extracted from cherries that most commonly ripen red but sometimes orange or yellow. The cherries are usually hand-picked then processed by various means. Sometimes they are dried in the fruit under tropical sunshine until they resemble raisins – a process known as 'natural'. The 'honey process' involves pulping the fresh cherries to extract the beans which are then sundried, still coated in their sticky mucilage. Alternatively, in the 'washed process', the freshly pulped beans are left to stand in tanks of water for several hours where enzyme activity breaks down the mucilage, before they are sundried on concrete patios or raised beds. Each method has a profound impact on the ultimate flavour of the coffee.

The term 'speciality coffee' is used to differentiate the world's best from the rest. This means it has to be Arabica, the species of coffee that is often bestowed with incredible flavours - unlike its hardy cousin Robusta which is usually reserved for commercial products and many instant blends. But being Arabica alone is by no means enough for a coffee to achieve the speciality tag, since the best beans are usually those grown at higher altitude on rich and fertile soils. As well as country and region of origin, the variety is important too; Bourbon, Typica, Caturra, Catuai, Pacamara and Geisha to name but a few. Just as Shiraz and Chardonnay grapes have their own complex flavours, the same is true of coffee's varieties. Some of the world's most amazing coffees are the result of the farmer's innovative approach to experimentation with growing and production techniques, meaning that today's speciality roaster is able to source coffees of incredible complexity and variation.

A good coffee establishment will showcase coffees when they are at their best – freshly harvested and seasonal, just like good fruit and vegetables. Seasonal espresso blends change throughout the year to reflect this.

As speciality coffee importers we source stand-out coffees by regularly travelling to origin countries. Direct trade with farmers is always our aim. Above all, we pay sustainable prices and encourage them to treat their land, and those who work it, with respect. Such an approach is increasingly demanded by London's speciality coffee community in order to safeguard the industry's future.

Photo: Alessandro Bonuzzi

191

Small Batch Roasting

by **Kurt Stewart**, Roaster and Co-owner, Volcano Coffee Works

I was brought up in a household dedicated to pickling, baking, sauce making and preserving. After experimenting with home brewing and wine making, my first foray into the aromatic world of small batch roasting was inevitable.

My own first experiments in small batch roasting started at home with some green beans and a wok. Of course roasting at home is much like home cooking, but when the term is applied to a commercial enterprise, it encompasses the passion and adventure of a home cook with the control and precision of a gourmet chef.

The art behind developing and building a roasting profile for a particular coffee is approached in the same way a chef develops cuisine, or a vintner crafts a wine. Culinary rules and science apply in equal measure. The roaster builds layers of flavour, working with the ingredients, sometimes pushing or manipulating the properties of an individual bean, to achieve the desired balance of sweetness, acidity, body, and the right mouth-feel and aftertaste. Coffee and wine share a vocabulary of descriptors, but as coffee has more flavour molecules than wine, coffee descriptors reach further into the culinary world. You will hear words describing aspects of flavour and taste senses, such as fruit acidity, sweet roundness, viscous syrup body, juicy plum, creamy, buttery, velvet chocolate textures. Delicious!

When a green bean is roasted, three fundamental processes occur that impact the flavours of the bean: enzyme by-products develop (giving the floral, citrus and fruity aromas), sugars brown (giving the sweet, caramel and nutty aromas), and plant fibres in the bean are roasted, known as dry-distillation (giving the spicy and smokey flavours). Only the enzyme by-products (which come from the coffee plant itself) are due to the bean chosen for roasting, whilst the remaining two processes are the result of how the bean is roasted. This is why no two small batch roasters will create an identical flavour profile from the same bean. Like chefs, each roaster will identify with, single out and highlight a flavour or combination of flavours which pleases, satisfies or amazes their palate.

Small Batch Roasting is a term reserved for those using roasting equipment controlled by the human hand rather than computers. A skilled roaster who understands his equipment, maintains ducting, understands heat/air ratios and extraction principles, coupled with following some basic fundamentals, can draw out origin characteristics and individual nuances, and create a roast where the optimum flavour potential is realised.

The roasting equipment itself is fundamentally a steel drum, which is usually heated by a gas flame. The drum constantly revolves, and at around 10 minutes of roasting at 203-205°C the developing beans reach 'first crack' (a bit like popcorn cracking). If roasting stops here, it will be a mild or lighter roast. When roasting continues, samples are taken with every revolution of the drum and the roaster observes the developing bean's colour, mass and aroma. The roaster may apply more or less heat or air and will remove the beans once they have reached the desired roast profile. This is usually within a 20 minute roasting time and often before second crack is reached as beyond this point the beans can lose their subtle origin characteristics and begin to take on a generic burnt flavour. The beans then enter the cooling tray until cool to touch. This process is in stark contrast to the large scale computer controlled commercial roasting process that takes between 90 seconds and 10 minutes at temperatures in excess of 360°C. The beans are then doused with water to cool them. Although this is the most economic way to roast beans, it takes away any

input by the roaster and does not give the bean enough time to develop fully.

When a roastery operation gets to such a scale that the roaster becomes distanced from their beans due to mechanised roasting processes and machinery, the instinct and hands-on effect that define a small batch roaster's product will always become somewhat diminished. And therein lies the excitement and diversity that small batch roasting offers over and above large-scale operations. It comes down to the physical ability of a talented roaster to exercise his or her senses, passion, enthusiasm, and the art of roasting.

Coffee Tasting

by **Lynsey Harley**, Founder, Modern Standard Coffee

C offee tasting is the process of identifying the characteristics of a particular coffee. In the coffee industry, professional 'cupping' sessions are conducted to evaluate coffees on a range of attributes. Cupping helps coffee buyers select which coffees to buy, and identify desirable attributes for formulating blends.

Coffee is most commonly scored using The Specialty Coffee Association of America (SCAA) system. Coffees achieving a score of 85 or higher (from a maximum of 100) are regarded as 'specialty' grade. These coffees have no defects and have a very distinct pleasant flavour profile. Coffees are scored on the following attributes: aroma, flavour, aftertaste, acidity, body, sweetness, cleanliness, uniformity and balance.

The cupping process follows a set procedure: 8.25g of coarsely ground coffee is measured into a shallow cup, specifically designed for the purpose. 150ml of water heated to 92˚C is added and left for 4 minutes. Next, a spoon is used to break and remove the 'crust', which provides the first opportunity to sample the coffee's aroma. After a further 6 minutes, the cupper begins to taste the coffee. Different attributes are evaluated at intervals as the coffee cools.

70˚C: Flavour and Aftertaste

Flavour: The coffee's principle flavour; what are your taste buds telling you?

Aftertaste: The length of positive flavour qualities after the coffee has been swallowed.

70˚C – 60˚C: Acidity and Body

Acidity: Bright for positive acidity, sour for negative. Positive acidity adds to the coffee's sweetness.

Body: The 'weight' of the brew. Is it heavy like a good red wine, or light and refined like a sauvignon blanc?

38˚C: Sweetness and Cleanliness.

Sweetness: Is the coffee sweet and pleasing?

Cleanliness: When no defects are found, the cup is clean.

Balance: Greater than the sum of its parts. Flavour, aftertaste, acidity and body work together to achieve balance.

One coffee can taste dramatically different depending on the processing method. Washing coffees increases the acidity, whilst the semi-washed process gives a honeyed sweetness to the coffee. The natural processing method can increase the sweetness, and can also encourage development of more obscure flavours including strawberry, blueberry and creamy notes.

Tasting coffee at home can be fun; exploring what a coffee can offer in terms of flavour, sweetness and other attributes is exciting. Your local speciality coffee shop can offer advice on which coffees are in season, and many will sell beans for you to experiment with at home. There's a coffee out there for everyone.

SCAA Coffee taster's wheel

Coffee Grinding

by **Jeremy Challender**, Co-owner and Director of Training, Prufrock Coffee and the

Grinder technology is about to change radically. Machine design, techniques behind the bar and hand brewing methodology have improved rapidly over recent years. Manufacturers are starting to address this by seeking feedback from users as well as lab testing. Home users can benefit from these changes too. New designs entering the market have drawn directly from the experiences of barista champions. Grinder designers are seeking professional and consumer feedback on taste, flavour and ergonomics through direct collaboration and field testing. Manufacturers are aware that we need development to continue and, now more than ever, baristas have a voice in this process. To be a barista in this time of grinder development is very exciting.

With all brew methods the challenge is replicating flavour and strength. Once we've got a precise brew recipe for a coffee we stand a better chance of extracting our coffee consistently. Commercially, the easiest way to navigate from this baseline towards the optimum extraction level is with micro-adjustments in the exposed surface area of the grinds — so the grinder is key to managing flavour in the cup.

The challenge grinder designers face is how to create consistency of grind size and shape. If you get out the microscope, and a set of test sieves, you start to realise all your grinds aren't the same size, nor are they all the same shape. If they were all the same size and shape, brewing would be much easier to control. In espresso you will have seen tiny granules in your cup that are smaller than the holes in the filter basket. We call these fines. These small particles have very high surface area and extract very quickly. As a home brewer, you could consider following the example of many championship baristas; invest in laboratory test sieves to remove a portion of particles under a certain size to reduce over-extracted flavours.

There is a portion of particles that fit side-on between the burrs and are planed rather than ground. We call these larger particles boulders. They have a much lower surface area relative to their size and in a 30 second espresso extraction will under-extract. Wobbly hand grinders are real offenders in the production of boulders. These too can be sieved out.

Sharp burrs are considered to reduce fines production. Ceramic burrs, which many hand grinders are fitted with, are very durable but are often not very sharp to start with. The material of choice at the moment is titanium-coated steel. Large burr diameter is linked to lower production of fines and boulders (more 'modal' distribution) so enormous bag grinders are being examined for application in espresso making. Cutting systems like spice grinders produce a very high proportion of fines and boulders, so are not recommended.

Keeping the coffee cool during grinding is a challenge. Burrs get hot in use because of friction, and some of the most exciting developments recently have focused on temperature stability of the burrs and burr casing with the addition of heating elements and fans. A warm grinder behaves differently to a cold or a hot one, so the particle shape and size are dependent on both grind setting and temperature.

Modern grinder design is very focussed on ease of access for regular cleaning. Arabica coffee has up to 17% fat content. We only extract a small percentage of this into a beverage but even after a day of commercial use, a grinder will have a slick of fats and tiny fine particles built up around the burr casing and the barrel and throat of the grinder. Oils oxidise, so grinders must be opened up and thoroughly swept out on a regular basis. Burrs can be washed in soapy water or coffee cleaner, or abrasive oil absorbing grinder cleaning granules can be used. Home baristas have an advantage here by being able to clean after a few shots rather than after a full day's usage.

The final hurdle to overcome is grind retention: many grinders on the market have large barrels and throats that can store as much as 40g of grinds that must be squeezed out before fresh grinds appear. At Prufrock, we are moving away from grinders with a high retention of grinds as we are looking to optimise freshness. When grind changes are required we want the benefit of micro-adjustment to be immediate. Here, home baristas are also well placed, as hand grinders have zero retention of grinds and some very high quality espresso hand grinders are now available on the market.

Over the last decade we have felt that machine technology has been in advance of grinders. We often comment that a barista's top priority should be the choice of grinder. Find a great grinding solution and great coffee will follow.

Photo: Jacob Thue

Espresso

by **Ben Townsend** Owner, The Espresso Room, and Trainer, London School of Coffee

The last 5 years have seen a rapid pace of development for coffee in London. The emergence of new cafes and roasteries continues apace as does the evolution of espresso technique. This "new world" culture is constantly pushing the boundaries of what is possible with the equipment, coffee and scientific knowledge that we currently have.

In a curious way, some of what is new is in fact quite old, and refers back to the largely disregarded tradition of Italian espresso. Of course, many practices remain deliberately different to traditional espresso — but it's instructive to note that the cutting edge of machine and grinder technology belongs again to the Italians, albeit achieved by recruiting non-Italian "new world" baristas to consult on the design.

Probably the most important series of changes over the last few years has been an increased understanding of grinding and extraction. Put simply, we can accurately measure with a laser refractometer how much of the desirable (or undesirable) soluble compounds in coffee have been extracted from the ground coffee by the brew water and the resulting effect on flavour.

To many people, notably espresso traditionalists, much London espresso has been unpalatably sour. We realise now that a combination of light roasting and short antipodean style shots has been severely underextracting our coffee, producing sour brews and overly simple flavour profiles.

All of London's serious cafes are now using brew recipes. A recipe describes per shot how much ground coffee goes in, how much liquid coffee comes out and over what time duration. Apart from allowing much more consistency from shot to shot, brew recipes are typically designed to produce as much sweetness and complexity as possible, without losing too much texture. We realise now that we should have been pushing more water through our coffee to extract more solubles and reduce sourness — the Italians have been doing this for decades!

I sincerely hope that we will not see the return of stale, over-roasted or Robusta coffee made on dirty machines. Traditional goals like thick crema on an espresso are very unreliable indicators of quality. The specialty scene has its colours firmly nailed to the mast of traceable, high quality, well processed and freshly roasted beans. Balanced, clean and fresh flavours that truly reveal the character of each coffee should be the goal of both barista and consumer.

Accordingly, it appears that the next wave of machine technology has finally lost the bewildering obsession with temperature and pressure control and moved onto technology to automate the brew recipe process. In practice, this means accurately dosing grinders and new "gravimetric" machines that cut the output of the shot using beverage mass instead of water volume or time. It will not be long before the weakest link in the physical production process will be the barista — a sobering thought!

The increased understanding of brew process and its resultant focus on brew recipes and extraction yield has turned scrutiny on roast profile. Those roasters producing the most soluble coffees, without baking or over-roasting, will be favoured by the best cafes.

We have also seen the emergence of a well-informed prosumer barista. Many home setups rival that of commercial cafes, and some home baristas are more technically informed than virtually all professional baristas, via internet blogs and some excellent new books.

When asked, I still advise that espresso is a drink to be enjoyed in a communal environment. For that reason I always go out for my flat whites and espresso. Coffee is about flavour, but not just that. It's an enjoyable route to shared social experience, whether you are leaning on a marble bar in Rome or a grungy wooden counter in Hackney.

Water - The Enigma

by **Maxwell Colonna-Dashwood**, Co-owner, Colonna and Small's, UK Barista Champion 2012 & 2014

This vital ingredient is the foundation of every cup of coffee you have ever tasted, apart from the bean itself of course.

It's not just coffee that relies so dramatically on this everyday and seemingly straightforward substance. The worlds of craft beer and whisky are suitable comparisons, with breweries and distilleries proudly signifying the provenance of their water as being a vital part of their product.

A roaster, though, sells coffee, the water bit comes post sale. The water will be different and unique based on the locality of brewing, and this is on top of all of the other variables that define coffee brewing such as grinding, temperature and brew ratios. The reality is that the impact of water is rarely directly witnessed, with the other variables often being seen as the cause for dramatic flavour changes. You may be wondering right now, how big an impact can it really have?

I'm yet to present the same coffee brewed with different waters to drinkers and not have them exclaim "I can't believe how different they are, they taste like different coffees'. These aren't "coffee people" either, but customers who contested prior to the tasting that "you may be able to taste the difference but I doubt I can tell."

It may make you question whether the coffee that you tried and weren't particularly keen on, was a representative version of what the bean actually tastes like, or at the least what it is capable of tasting of like.

So, why the big difference, what is in the water?

Nearly all water that trickles out of a tap or sits in a bottle is not just water. As well as the H2O there are other bits and bobs in the water. Minerals mainly. These have a big impact not only on what we extract from the coffee but also how that flavour sits in the cup of coffee.

It's fair to say that currently the way the coffee industry discusses water is through the use of a measurement called Total Dissolved Solids (TDS).

TDS has become the measurement which is relied upon to distinguish and inform us about how water will affect our coffee. It gives us a total of everything in the water. The problem though, is that TDS doesn't tell us everything we need to know about the water; it doesn't tell us about what those solids are. On top of this, TDS meters don't measure some non-solids that have a huge impact on flavour.

In the water, we need the minerals calcium and magnesium to help pull out a lot of the desirable flavour in the coffee, but we also need the right amount of buffering ability in the water to balance the acids. This buffering ability can be noted as the bicarbonate content of the water. So for example an "empty" soft water with no minerals will lack flavour complexity and the lack of buffer will mean a more vinegary acidity.

A good test is to make the same coffee with both Evian and Tesco Ashbeck water. Evian has a good amount of calcium and magnesium to pull flavour out, but this is accompanied by a high bicarbonate content which flattens everything out and results in a heavy, bitter and chalky brew. The Ashbeck has little extraction power so is quite empty but has a low buffer so the acidity verges on sour. For bottled waters, Waitrose Essential yields pleasant results.

However the coffee shops in this guide will most likely have a trick up their sleeve. The industry filtration systems that have been developed primarily to stop scale build up in the striking and valuable espresso machines, also produce water compositions that are more often than not preferable for coffee brewing. Speciality coffee shops require all manner of specifics to be obsessed over and carefully executed. That cup of coffee that hits you and stops you in your step with intense, balanced and complex flavour will owe its brilliance to careful brewing, a knowledgeable brewer and superb equipment. However, it also owes a significant part of its beautiful character and flavour to the water it is brewed with.

Brewing Filter Coffee at Home

by **Christian Baker, David Robson & Sam Mason**

Y ou may be surprised to know that filter coffee brewed at home can rival that of your favourite coffee shop. All you need is good quality ingredients and some inexpensive equipment. Keep in mind that small variations in grind coarseness, coffee / water ratio and brew time will make a significant difference to flavour, and that trial and error is the key to unlocking perfection.

Whole Beans: Whole bean coffee is superior to pre-ground. Coffee rapidly deteriorates once ground, so buy your coffee in whole bean form and store it in an air-tight container at room temperature. It should be consumed between three and thirty days after roast and ground only moments before brewing.

Water: Water is important because it makes up over 98% of the finished drink. Only use bottled water, preferably with a dry residue between 80-150mg/l. London tap water is not suitable for brewing - it will inhibit your ability to extract flavour and reveal only a fraction of a coffee's potential.

Digital scales: Get a set of scales accurate to 1g and large enough to hold your coffee brewer. Coffee is commonly measured in 'scoops' or 'tablespoons', but coffee and water are best measured by weight for greater accuracy and to ensure repeatability. Small changes in the ratio of coffee to water can have a significant impact on flavour. A good starting point is 60-70g of coffee per litre of water. Apply this ratio to meet the size of your brewer.

Grinder

A burr grinder is essential. Burr grinders are superior to blade grinders because they allow the grind coarseness to be set and produce a more consistent size of coffee fragment (critical for an even extraction). As a general rule, the coarser the grind the longer the brew time required, and vice versa. For example, an espresso needs a very fine grind whereas a French Press works with a coarser grind.

French Press

Preheat the French Press with hot water, and discard. Add 34g of coarsely ground coffee and pour in 500g of water just below boiling point (94/95°C). Steep for 4 to 5 minutes then gently plunge to the bottom. Decant the coffee straight away to avoid over-brewing (known as over-extraction).

AeroPress

The AeroPress is wonderfully versatile. It can be used with finely ground coffee and a short steep time, or with a coarser grind and a longer steep time. The latter is our preferred method for its flavour and repeatability. Preheat the AeroPress using hot water, and discard. Rinse the paper filter before securing, and place the AeroPress over a sturdy cup or jug. Add 16g of coffee and pour in 240g of water at 95°C. Secure the plunger on top, creating a seal. Steep for 3 minutes then plunge over 20 seconds.

Pour Over

We recommend using a pouring kettle for better pouring control. Place a filter paper in the cone and rinse through with hot water. Add 15g of coffee and slowly pour 30g of 95°C water to pre-soak the coffee grounds. This creates the 'bloom'. After 30 seconds add 250g of water, pouring steadily in a circular motion over the centre. It should take 1 minute and 45 seconds to pour and between 30-45 seconds to drain through. The key is to keep the flow of water steady. If the water drains too quickly/slowly, adjust the coarseness of the grind to compensate.

Stovetop

A stovetop will not make an espresso, it will, however, make a strong coffee. Pour hot water in to the base to the fill-line or just below the pressure release valve. Fill the basket with ground coffee of medium coarseness (between Pour Over and French Press). Traditional wisdom suggests a fine grind in pursuit of espresso, but stovetops extract differently to espresso machines and grinding fine is a recipe for bitter, over-extracted coffee. Screw the base to the top and place on the heat. When you hear bubbling, remove immediately and decant to ensure the brewing has stopped.

Illustrations: Zoë Barker

MAKING ONE PERSON SMILE CAN CHANGE THE WORLD. MAYBE NOT THE WHOLE WORLD, BUT THEIR WORLD.

CLEAN DRINKING WATER IS A BASIC HUMAN RIGHT WHICH EVERY PERSON IN THE WORLD SHOULD HAVE ACCESS TO. DESPITE THIS, 738 MILLION PEOPLE CURRENTLY TRY TO SURVIVE WITHOUT IT.

Spread the smile by taking part in UK Coffee Week 2015 (4 - 10 May) and supporting Project Waterfall in participating coffee shops nationwide. To find out more, visit www.ukcoffeeweek.com

To learn more about our latest project in the Amhara region of Ethiopia, visit www.allegrafoundation.org

#SPREADTHESMILE

Education & Training

by **Edwin Harrison**, Co-owner, the Artisan Coffee School

The London third wave coffee scene is well established and thriving. So let's look behind the coffee machines for a moment to better understand what impact education and training has on your daily cup of coffee. Making coffee is a complex art and science; any number of small variables, from plantation to barista, can make the difference between a mouthwatering cup and one that ends up being poured down the drain. Owners and managers spend hours focusing on training in order to drive their coffee shops forward and do justice to the coffee growers, roasters and other professionals who have in some way contributed to delivering those amazing beans to our grinder hoppers.

To understand where coffee training and education has arrived today, it's useful to take a brief look at its history. The explosion of branded coffee shop chains in the 1990s lead to the birth of the barista manual, Manuals served to formalise training, systems and techniques by introducing a workflow process for baristas to follow. Together with mass training sessions, the barista manual successfully addressed problems of inconsistency and the coffee chains flourished, but little progress was made to realise coffee's full potential.

The complexity and potential of coffee was too great to be boxed up into a manual or process; the third wave independents were eager to take coffee to the next level. Top baristas started to get excited about what could be achieved through experimentation; everything from milk texturing to coffee flavour profiles came under meticulous scrutiny. Baristas challenged conventional wisdom and investigated the science behind coffee making to understand how it could be improved. Today a new breed of dedicated training schools has emerged exploring coffee theory as well as practical brewing skills. What's more, coffee schools are no longer the preserve of industry professionals, they now offer classes tailored specifically to interested coffee lovers wishing to improve their home brewing.

An introductory barista course run over one or two days would typically include theory with a discussion on processing techniques, different roast types, and establish what flavours we are looking to achieve. The white board will then turn into something you would expect to see in an in-depth physics presentation as coffee enthusiasts discover how to create their own brew ratio. This process alone indicates just how much influence the barista has over the coffee they produce.

Then it's on to the machine, working out variables and learning how to keep these consistent is fundamental to success. Exploring extraction times, tamping and grind adjustments are just some of the many aspects covered and the trainer will always bring it back to what impact your actions have on the flavour of the coffee. This is key to developing a deeper knowledge of the process you are responsible for. This approach to training becomes infectious as suddenly the world of coffee begins to unfold in front of students' eyes. This is why we see so many students progress from the barista foundation courses through to intermediate and professional level.

The industry as a whole has stepped up and taken notice of this revolution in education. The Speciality Coffee Association of Europe (SCAE) addressed the wide gap in formalised training, gathering top industry figures to formalise a structure with inspiration from the wine industry. The result is the Coffee Diploma System, taking a modular form incorporating the many different aspects of coffee education, and assessed with exams. Many coffee schools, offer SCAE accredited courses in addition to running their own classes. The rise of coffee schools demonstrates that the industry is taking the next big step and realising that barista training is not a single shadow shift at the start of a job, but an ongoing process that has a very significant impact on the success of a business; from staff retention to the consistency and quality of coffee they serve.

Coffee Glossary

Acidity: the pleasant tartness of a coffee. Examples of acidity descriptors include lively and flat. One of the principal attributes evaluated by professional tasters when determining the quality of a coffee.

AeroPress: a hand-powered coffee brewer marketed by Aerobie Inc., and launched in 2005. Consists of two cylinders, one sliding within the other, somewhat resembling a large syringe. Water is forced through ground coffee held in place by a paper filter, creating a concentrated filter brew.

Affogato: one or more scoops of vanilla ice cream topped with a shot of espresso, served as a dessert.

Americano, Caffè Americano: a long coffee consisting of espresso with hot water added on top. Originates from the style of coffee favoured by American GIs stationed in Europe during WWII.

Arabica, Coffea arabica: the earliest cultivated species of coffee tree and the most widely grown, Arabica accounts for approximately 70% of the world's coffee. Superior in quality to Robusta, it is more delicate and is generally grown at higher altitudes.

Aroma: the fragrance produced by brewed coffee. Examples of aroma descriptors include earthy, spicy and floral. One of the principal attributes evaluated by professional tasters when determining the quality of a coffee.

Barista: a professional person skilled in making coffee, particularly one working at an espresso bar.

Blend: a combination of coffees from different countries or regions. Mixed together, they achieve a balanced flavour profile no single coffee can offer alone.

Body: describes the heaviness, thickness or relative weight of coffee on the tongue. One of the principal attributes evaluated by professional tasters when determining quality of a coffee.

Bottomless portafilter, naked portafilter: a portafilter without spouts, allowing espresso to flow directly from the bottom of the filter basket into the cup. Allows the extraction to be monitored visually.

Brew group: the assembly protruding from the front of an espresso machine consisting of the grouphead, portafilter and basket. The brew group must be heated to a sufficient temperature to produce a good espresso.

Brew pressure: pressure of 9 bar is required for espresso extraction.

Brew temperature: the water temperature at the point of contact with coffee. Optimum brew temperature varies by extraction method. Espresso brew temperature is typically 90-95˚C. A stable brew temperature is crucial for good espresso.

Brew time, extraction time: the contact time between water and coffee. Espresso brew time is typically 25-30 seconds. Brew times are dictated by a variety of factors including the grind coarseness and degree of roast.

Burr set: an integral part of a coffee grinder. Consists of a pair of rotating steel discs between which coffee beans are ground. Burrs are either flat or conical in shape.

Café con leche: a traditional Spanish coffee consisting of espresso topped with scalded milk.

Caffeine: an odourless, slightly bitter alkaloid responsible for the stimulating effect of coffee.

Cappuccino: a classic Italian coffee comprising espresso, steamed milk and topped with a layer of foam. Traditionally served in a 6oz cup and sometimes topped with powdered chocolate or cinnamon.

Capsule: a self-contained, pre-ground, pre-pressed portion of coffee, individually sealed inside a plastic capsule. Capsule brewing systems are commonly found in domestic coffee machines. Often compatible only with certain equipment brands.

Chemex: A type of pour over coffee brewer with a distinctive hourglass-shaped vessel. Invented in 1941, the Chemex has become regarded as a design classic and is on permanent display at the Museum of Modern Art in New York City.

Cherry: the fruit of the coffee plant. Each cherry contains two coffee seeds (beans).

Cortado: a traditional short Spanish coffee consisting of espresso cut with a small quantity of steamed milk. Similar to an Italian piccolo.

Crema: the dense caramel-coloured layer that forms on the surface of an espresso. Consists of emulsified oils created by the dispersion of gases in liquid at high pressure. The presence of crema is commonly equated with a good espresso.

Cupping: a method by which professional tasters perform sensory evaluation of coffee. Hot water is poured over ground coffee and left to extract. The taster first samples the aroma, then tastes the coffee by slurping it from a spoon.

Decaffeinated: coffee with approximately 97% or more of its naturally occurring caffeine removed is classified as decaffeinated.

Dispersion screen, shower screen: a component of the grouphead that ensures even distribution of brewing water over the coffee bed in the filter basket.

Dosage: the mass of ground coffee used for a given brewing method. Espresso dosage is typically 7-10g of ground coffee (14-20g for a double).

Double espresso, doppio: typically 30-50ml extracted from 14-20g of ground coffee. The majority of coffee venues in this guide serve double shots as standard.

Drip method: a brewing method that allows brew water to seep through a bed of ground coffee by gravity, not pressure.

Espresso: the short, strong shot of coffee that forms the basis for many other coffee beverages. Made by forcing hot water at high pressure through a compressed bed of finely ground coffee.

Espresso machine: in a typical configuration, a pump delivers hot water from a boiler to the brew group, where it is forced under pressure through ground coffee held in the portafilter. A separate boiler delivers steam for milk steaming.

Extraction: the process of infusing coffee with hot water to release flavour, accomplished either by allowing ground coffee to sit in hot water for a period of time or by forcing hot water through ground coffee under pressure.

Filter method: any brewing method in which water filters through a bed of ground coffee.

Coffee Glossary contd.

Most commonly used to describe drip method brewers that use a paper filter to separate grounds from brewed coffee.

Flat white: an espresso-based beverage first made popular in Australia and New Zealand. Made with a double shot of espresso with finely steamed milk and a thin layer of microfoam. Typically served as a 5-6oz drink with latte art.

Flavour: the way a coffee tastes. Flavour descriptors include nutty and earthy. One of the principal attributes evaluated by professional tasters when determining the quality of a coffee.

French press, plunger pot, cafetiere: a brewing method that separates grounds from brewed coffee by pressing them to the bottom of the brewing receptacle with a mesh filter attached to a plunger.

Froth, foam: created when milk is heated and aerated, usually with hot steam from an espresso machine's steam wand. Used to create a traditional cappuccino.

Green coffee, green beans: unroasted coffee. The dried seeds from the coffee cherry.

Grind: the degree of coarseness to which coffee beans are ground. A crucial factor in determining the nature of a coffee brew. Grind coarseness should be varied in accordance with the brewing method. Methods involving longer brew times call for a coarse grind. A fine grind is required for brew methods with a short extraction time such as espresso.

Grinder: a vital piece of equipment for making coffee. Coffee beans must be ground evenly for a good extraction. Most commonly motorised, but occasionally manual. Burr grinders are the best choice for an even grind.

Group: see Brew Group

Grouphead: a component of the brew group containing the locking connector for the portafilter and the dispersion screen.

Honey process, pulped natural, semi-washed: a method of processing coffee where the cherry is removed (pulped), but the beans are sun-dried with mucilage intact. Typically results in a sweet flavour profile with a balanced acidity.

Latte, caffè latte: an Italian beverage made with espresso combined with steamed milk, traditionally topped with foamed milk and served in a glass. Typically at least 8oz in volume, usually larger.

Latte art: the pattern or design created by pouring steamed milk on top of espresso. Only finely steamed milk is suitable for creating latte art. Popular patterns include the rosetta and heart.

Lever espresso machine: lever machines use manual force to drive a piston that generates the pressure required for espresso extraction. Common in the first half of the 20th century, but now largely superseded by electric pump-driven machines. Lever machines retain a small but passionate group of proponents.

Long black: a coffee beverage made by adding an espresso on top of hot water. Similar to an Americano, but usually shorter and the crema is preserved.

Macchiato: a coffee beverage consisting of espresso 'stained' with a dash of steamed milk (espresso macchiato) or a tall glass of steamed milk 'stained' with espresso (latte macchiato).

Macrofoam: stiff foam containing large bubbles used to make a traditional cappuccino. Achieved by incorporating a greater quantity of air during the milk steaming process.

Microfoam: the preferred texture of finely-steamed milk for espresso-based coffee drinks. Essential for pouring latte art. Achieved by incorporating a lesser quantity of air during the milk steaming process.

Micro-lot coffee: coffee originating from a small, discrete area within a farm, typically benefiting from conditions favourable to the development of a particular set of characteristics. Micro-lot coffees tend to fetch higher prices due to their unique nature.

Mocha, caffè mocha: similar to a caffè latte, but with added chocolate syrup or powder.

Natural process: a simple method of processing coffee where whole cherries (with the bean inside) are dried on raised beds under the sun. Typically results in a lower acidity coffee with a heavier body and exotic flavours.

Over extracted: describes coffee with a bitter or burnt taste, resulting from ground coffee exposed to hot water for too long.

Peaberry: a small, round coffee bean formed when only one seed, rather than the usual two, develops in a coffee cherry. Peaberry beans produce a different flavour profile, typically lighter-bodied with higher acidy.

Piccolo: a short Italian coffee beverage made with espresso topped with an equal quantity of steamed milk. Traditionally served in a glass.

Pod: a self-contained, pre-ground, pre-pressed puck of coffee, individually wrapped inside a perforated paper filter. Mostly found in domestic espresso machines. Often compatible only with certain equipment brands.

Pour over: a type of drip filter method in which a thin, steady stream of water is poured slowly over a bed of ground coffee contained within a filter cone.

Pouring kettle: a kettle with a narrow swan-neck spout specifically designed to deliver a steady, thin stream of water.

Portafilter: consists of a handle (usually plastic) attached to a metal cradle that holds the filter basket. Inserted into the group head and locked in place in preparation for making an espresso. Usually features a single or double spout on the underside to direct the flow of coffee into a cup.

Portafilter basket: a flat bottomed, bowl-shaped metal insert that sits in the portafilter and holds a bed of ground coffee. The basket has an array of tiny holes in the base allowing extracted coffee to seep through and pour into a cup.

Puck: immediately after an espresso extraction, the bed of spent coffee grounds forms compressed waste matter resembling a small hockey puck.

Pull: the act of pouring an espresso. The term originates from the first half of the 20th century when manual machines were the norm, and baristas pulled a lever to create an espresso.

Ristretto: a shorter 'restricted' shot of espresso. Made using the same dose and brew time as for a regular espresso, but with less water. The result is a richer and more intense beverage.

Coffee Glossary contd.

Roast: the process by which green coffee is heated in order to produce coffee beans ready for consumption. Caramelisation occurs as intense heat converts starches in the bean to simple sugars, imbuing the bean with flavour and transforming its colour to a golden brown.

Robusta, Coffea canephora: the second most widely cultivated coffee species after arabica, robusta accounts for approximately 30% of the world's coffee. Robusta is hardier and grown at lower altitudes than arabica. It has a much higher caffeine content than arabica, and a less refined flavour. Commonly used in instant coffee blends.

Shot: a single unit of brewed espresso.

Single origin, single estate: coffee from one particular region or farm.

Siphon brewer, vacuum brewer: an unusual brewing method that relies on the action of a vacuum to draw hot water through coffee from one glass chamber to another. The resulting brew is remarkably clean.

Small batch: refers to roasting beans in small quantities, typically between 4-24kg, but sometimes larger.

Speciality coffee: a premium quality coffee scoring 80 points or above (from a total of 100) in the SCAA grading scale.

Steam wand: the protruding pipe found on an espresso machine that supplies hot steam used to froth and steam milk.

Stovetop, moka pot: a brewing method that makes strong coffee (but not espresso). Placed directly on a heat source, hot water is forced by steam pressure from the lower chamber to the upper chamber, passing through a bed of coffee.

Tamp: the process of distributing and pressing ground coffee into a compact bed within the portafilter basket in preparation for brewing espresso. The degree of pressure applied during tamping is a key variable in espresso extraction. Too light and the brew water will percolate rapidly (tending to under extract), too firm and the water flow will be impeded (tending to over extract).

Tamper: the small pestle-like tool used to distribute and compact ground coffee in the filter basket.

Third wave coffee: the movement that treats coffee as an artisanal foodstuff rather than a commodity product. Quality coffee reflects its terroir, in a similar manner to wine.

Under extracted: describes coffee that has not been exposed to brew water for long enough. The resulting brew is often sour and thin-bodied.

V60: a popular type of pour over coffee brewer marketed by Hario. The product takes its name from the 60° angle of the V-shaped cone. Typically used to brew one or two cups only.

Washed process: one of the most common methods of processing coffee cherries. Involves fermentation in tanks of water to remove mucilage. Typically results in a clean and bright flavour profile with higher acidity.

Whole bean: coffee that has been roasted but not ground.

A-Z List of Coffee Venues

A-Z List of Coffee Venues contd.